# STOCK MARKET INVESTING FOR BEGINNERS 2021

## *A Simplified Beginner's Guide To Starting Investing In The Stock Market And Achieve Your Financial Freedom*

*Nathan Bell*

## Disclaimer

All erudition supplied in this book is specified for educational and academic purposes only. The author is not in any way in charge of any outcomes that emerge from using this book. Constructive efforts have been made to render information that is both precise and effective; however, the author is not to be held answerable for the accuracy or use/misuse of this information.

## Foreword

I will like to thank you for taking the very first step of trusting me and deciding to purchase/read this life-transforming book. Thanks for investing your time and resources on this product.

I can assure you of precise outcomes if you will diligently follow the specific blueprint I lay bare in the information handbook you are currently checking out. It has transformed lives, and I firmly believe it will equally change your own life too.

All the information I provided in this Do It Yourself piece is easy to absorb and practice.

## Table of Contents

## INTRODUCTION

Before you study how you can turn the stock market into a goldmine, you should first have an excellent foundation of the fundamentals of investing in stocks. Stock Investing has been an honor for me to write. I'm grateful that I can share my knowledge, information, and experience with such a devoted and large group of readers.

Although the stock market has served countless financiers for nearly a century, recent years have shown me that an excellent investing lorry such as stocks can be quickly misunderstood, misused, and even mistreated.

Recently, millions of investors lost an overall of over 5 trillion dollars. Financiers at the tail end of a bull market frequently think that stock investing is a secure, carefree, specific method to make a fast riches. The many stories of investors who lost improbable quantities of cash hypothesizing in tech stocks, dot-.coms, and other fancy stocks are lessons for everyone. Successful stock investing takes thorough work and knowledge like any other significant prematch. This book can help you prevent the mistakes others have made and can point you in the right direction.

# CHAPTER ONE

## Stock Market

A stock market, to say the least, is a place for trading stocks. It also functions as a sign of the financial cycle. When the economy is performing well, the prices of commodities tend to increase in the market, typically. When the economy is down, the costs of stocks also decrease; this can be true even for a very high share. It is also worth noting that the costs of stocks mainly depend on the efficiency of a business. When a company is succeeding, the price of its stocks will also tend to increase; the opposite would take place if the business is not earning well. There are odd cases where speculators are buying stock that is not performing well at all, which will result in a high stock cost even for a lousy business, but that is another story for another time. Now, the question is: Why using stocks? The reason is that it assists businesses to raise funds to finance their tasks, whether for the expansion of the company, or for their day-to-day activities, or just to please their stakeholders. Money, after all, is the brain behind every investment.

## Stock

A stock, also known to as a share, represents ownership of a business. When you purchase stocks from a company, you get to work out ownership rights of the company, for instance, a claim on the company's properties and revenues, and ballot rights. Remember that there are different kinds of stocks. When you see investors talking about the stock market, they usually refer to a typical stock.

Stock Market Index

You might hear them talk about how the market increases or falls one day when individuals talk about stocks. The way to view this is to know the stock market index or indices.

There are many stocks present in the stock exchange. Similar stocks are grouped to form an index.

Having an index is an excellent way to sort the various kinds of stocks in the market. After all, the stock exchange is composed of several stocks. It will be confused if you fail to sort similar stocks in the same place. It is also a thing of reference for contrast. You can compare the tendency of the index worth with the pattern of the cost of specific stocks that fit into that same index. You can as well compare one index with another and see which industry might be a rewarding investment.

Considering that there are many stocks in the market, and the index can sort all of them out in an orderly manner, an index acts as a good representation of the whole market. If you look at the index of the IT industry, then you will know the average performance of the stocks in the IT market. This applies to other markets. There are different ways to make contrasts, depending on how the shares are arranged in an index.

How the stocks are organized together identifies the type of category of the index. For instance, in a world stock market index, such as in the S&P Global 100, you will discover stocks that are found worldwide. These are stocks from different countries in the world, such as Asia and Europe. There is also what is known as the national index.

As the name suggests, this type of index considers the performance of the stock market in a particular country. You can likewise discover a more specific index that reveals the habits of the stock market on a local level. When analyzing the stock market, it is advisable to study various indexes so that you can have a much better understanding of what is truly going on in the stock market.

## Long-Term versus Short-Term Stock

You can choose how long you want to purchase the stock market. Many traders invest just in one day. Therefore they are known as day traders, but it is also typical to discover people who purchase stocks for more than five years. This depends on your preference, along with how you want to approach the stock market. When to categorize an investment as a short- term or long term, there is no quick and challenging guideline for that. Some financial investments start as a short term but then grow into a long time while doing so. For beginners, the majority of people specify a short-term investment as any investment that lasts for a year. For this reason, all other investments that lasted for more than one year are considered as a long-lasting investment. Again, such meaning is approximately you.

It is worth noting that the stock exchange, in general, does not fluctuate too quickly. You can not anticipate a significant return on a short-term investment as much as you can get from a lucrative long-term investment. Numerous short-term investments only last for a month or some months.

The problem with long-lasting investing is that it is more difficult to predict how the market will respond during your investment. Even though the market is doing terrible now, it can do well after a year. Of course, the difference can take place.

The purpose of the investment also matters. If you desire to save for retirement, then a long-term investment is the best.

It is to be noted that the market takes some time to respond. This is among the issues why day trading might not be the right choice considering that the market might take more than 24 hours before it reacts to your prediction. Another separating factor is the technique that you change. For short-term savings, technical analysis would be valuable to you; however, for a long-term investment, the fundamental analysis would be the much better option.

## Stock Investing versus Trading

It is rather safe to state that there is no difference between investing in and trading stocks. A view drawn from a fundamental perspective, they are interchangeable. Nevertheless, for the word Nazis out there, investing and trading stocks might have some distinctions.

You can trade many stocks on a single day. On the other hand, investing means a less active approach where you purchase particular shares and hold on to them for a more extended period so that you can sell them later for a profit.

Remember that this book uses both words synonymously with no reference to any practical implication. After all, before you can buy anything, you first need to have money to purchase your goods. And, when you buy stocks, you also need to sell and trade them afterward for you to earn an income. Short-term investing likewise consists of the habits of day traders who trade stocks within a single day.

Is it for you?
Anybody can invest in stocks; this type of investment is not for everybody. You have to earn it if making revenue is your

intention (which should always be). Real expert financiers spend hours of research and study regularly. Yes, you can earn money in the stock market by just relying on mere luck without any investigation. But, you cannot expect to make a continuous profit by merely relying on mere luck or guesswork.

To make the stock market a rewarding place for you and your company, you require to devote severe time and effort into discovering the craft of investing in stocks. This indicates that you need to be ready to spend hours of research study and be sure you are following the stock market on a routine basis.

## Fundamentals Of The Stock Market

Owners of business have been raising capital through the sale of equity interests for many years. But the auction of equity interests via a public market dates back more detailed to four-hundred years.

In the early 1600s, a Dutch shipping business sold shares of itself to increase the capital it required to broaden business operations. Other companies began offering shares of themselves for sale, and innovative business owners started trading commodities, stocks, and other monetary instruments in personal markets. A stock market opened in Amsterdam in 1611 in response to the increase in the trading of products and financial securities. Over the next couple of centuries, other markets opened in Europe only.

In the year 1792, brokers assemble under a buttonwood tree in Wall Street to formulate rules for buying and selling stocks and bonds-- the precursor to the New York Stock Exchange. The following bullet points will tell you enough about the most crucial exchanges, so everyone will not assume you're checking out Wall Street for the first time.

- -American Stock Exchange (AMEX)-- For some years, the smallest of the three primary U.S. stock markets. The American Stock Exchange, frequently called Amex, offered itself to NYSE Euronext in 2008. While the mom's and dad's business changed Amex's name to NYSE MKT, the old name has remained. This exchange centers on small-cap stocks, exchange-traded funds, and derivatives.
- -Chicago Board Options Exchange (CBOE)-- The world's largest market for choices on stocks, indexes, and interest rates.

- -Chicago Mercantile Exchange (CME)-- The country's largest futures exchange, and the second most prominent worldwide.
- -Nasdaq Stock Market (NASDAQ)-- Commonly called just the Nasdaq; this market is a subsidiary of Nasdaq OMX Group, which operates 24 markets on six continents.
- -New York Stock Exchange (NYSE)-- The earliest, and some state still the most prominent, stock exchange in the United States. The NYSE is a subsidiary of NYSE Euronext, an international conglomerate that controls those markets that sell more than 8,000 equities and account for nearly 40% of the world's stock trading.

Most big companies and many little ones trade on exchanges to make it easier for investors to buy their shares. Exchangers need the business to satisfy specific criteria, such as the variety of shares readily available, market cap, share price, and financial rules, before they will note the stock for trading. However, thousands of companies do not list their stocks on exchanges either because they can't satisfy the listing requirements or merely choose not to pay the exchanges' charges. Those stocks trade via networks of securities dealerships who work out deals among themselves. Such stocks are said to be OTC or buy on-the-counter.

As OTC stocks tend to be small and less accessible than those that trade on exchanges, they have obtained a reputation for threat. Naturally, lots of OTC stocks make suitable investments and lots of big foreign business trade non-prescription. Novices, nevertheless, might want to steer clear of OTC stocks, particularly cent stocks-- stocks that trade at meager rates.

Both exchanges and OTC markets welcome foreign companies. Companies situated outside the United States can sign up American depositary receipts (ADRs) or other customized securities that sell their stocks on U.S. exchanges. Various U.S. companies take advantage of comparable systems to trade on markets in Canada, Europe, or Asia. Not before having financiers delighted in such flexibility to buy and sell securities.

## What You Should Know

Once you start investing or even looking into investments, you'll likely encounter different terms specialists in the field anticipate you to know. If you read about the Wall Street Journal or enjoy CNBC, reporters will frequently toss around expressions like "bull market" and "penny stocks" without specifying them. If you don't know what you encounter in the financial media or something your broker tells you, ask for an explanation or check the term above. Don't be ashamed of your lack of knowledge. Ignorance can be dangerous to your success, and smart investors won't buy anything or fill out a form, answer a personal question, or make a monetary pledge until they know the consequences of their actions.

The exchange names provided above are a good start when it comes to learning the vocabulary of investment.

## Q&A-- Important Questions

There is more to investing than memorizing many terms. For answers to 10 questions that beginner stock investors typically ask, keep reading.

Question # 1: How do I start capitalizing in stocks exchange?

Answer: Open an investment account with a stockbroker. While some companies allow you to purchase your first share of stock directly from them, most businesses trade their shares just on dealer networks or through stock exchanges. A brokerage account will give you a chance to access many stocks and shared funds and other financial investments.

Question # 2: How much do I need to start buying stocks?

Answer: In an ideal world, you'll jump into the market with $100,000-- enough to purchase a diversified portfolio of stocks at once. Even if you can spare just $5,000 or $1,000, you can still invest in stocks.

Naturally, limiting yourself to just one business's stock, or small stocks call for danger. However, while you handle some risk when you purchase only one or two shares, choosing not to invest exposes you to another kind of threat-- poverty.

If you have an account at a discount broker charging $10 per trade, acquiring $1,000 in stock will cost you 1 percent of your income in commissions. That means your inventory must return about 1% before you recover the expense of the investment. As a guideline, investors should try to minimize their charge costs below 0.5% of the portfolio worth for the year. As the collection grows, your investment commissions should reduce as a percentage of the resources (See Table below).

| Portfolio size | Cost to build 20-stock portfolio @ $10 per trade | % of portfolio | Cost to build 20-stock portfolio @ $50 per trade | % of portfolio |
|---|---|---|---|---|
| $50,000 | $200 | 0.40% | $1,000 | 2.00% |
| $100,000 | $200 | 0.20% | $1,000 | 1.00% |
| $500,000 | $200 | 0.04% | $1,000 | 0.20% |

Table 1.0-- Errors of Commission

If you have $1,000 to invest, leap, and pay the commission. You've got to begin somewhere. You'll be including new cash to the account over time if you dedicate to investing. Invest some years enjoying your stocks increase in worth, and after a while, the commissions will not take such a huge bite out of the whole.

Question # 3: I want to purchase Apple, but the stock expenses any dollars per share, and I don't have enough cash to buy 100 shares. Should I stick to cheaper stocks?

Answer 1: This concern needs two responses. Relating to the question of buying 100 shares. Some decades back, purchase shares in great round deals of 100 count. Brokers do not like dealing with smaller trades, and often they charged lower commissions for round lots. Some full-service brokers still choose to handle round lots, however with securities trading digitally and discount brokers charging a fixed rate for many trades, today, you can purchase eighty-seven shares of Stock A and forty-two shares of Stock B, without encountering a tough time.

Dollar-based investing centers on the size of the stock point in dollars, not shares. Think about putting $2,500 in each stock, which relates to fifty shares of $50 stock, eighty-three shares of $30 stock, or twenty-nine shares of an $80 stock. Holding equivalent dollar of all your stocks not just minimizes the threat in lopsided portfolios (if your highest holding falls, it triggers an out of proportion decrease in the worth of your whole collection), but also makes it easier to examine how your stocks are performing.

Answer 2: The second answer addresses the problem of cheap stocks. Many financiers, particularly those who began buying stocks during the days when everybody bought shares in round lots, still see a $100 inventory as more expensive than a $50 stock. Experts value stocks relative to revenues, money flows, or sales, and so should you do.

Question # 4: Which one should I purchase, bonds, or stocks?

Answer: For many investors, the intelligent answer is both. Both bonds and stocks play an essential role in a portfolio. While stocks offer superior development capacity throughout good years (in addition to many drawback potentials during bad years), bonds provide higher income and steadier general returns (though they can't match stocks for possible advantage).

While not all stocks follow the same path, they do tend to relocate comparable instructions. If the S&P 500 Index has returned 15% in a particular year, for example, many stocks-- even those outside the index-- have most likely published positive returns. Some tread more quickly than others, naturally.

Bonds also tend to relocate the same instructions as other bonds. However, different classes within the bond group (such as long-term business bonds, Treasury expenses, high-yield bonds, and so on) will see their incomesdeviate.

While bonds and stocks tend to run in loose packs, a reality investors ought to use to lower volatility is that those packs do not frequently run together. How much should you put in stocks against bonds? The equation means a 30-year-old must hold 80% stocks and 20% bonds, while an 80-year-old needs to hold 30% stocks and 70% bonds.

Question # 5: How do I know the stocks to buy?

Answer: Whole books have been written on this subject, however most stock analysis comes down to a few key styles:

**Worth.**

Even the fastest-growing stock is not worth buying if you have to pay too much. Beginners, in particular, should not mess around with expensive hyper growth stocks. Before you buy, think about the stock's key valuation ratios (price/earnings and operating money circulation).

**Growth.**

If the business can't increase its earnings, even the least expensive stock isn't worth purchasing. Rising sales, revenues, and cash flow recommend the company's products sell well enough to increase its penetration of the market.

**Success.**

Any business can grow if it spends enough cash. A well-run business can keep their profit margins while still growing.

Investors should target stocks with steady or increasing success.

**News.**

What type of headings does the stock create? Both great news and problem can impact a stock's price before any changes drip down to the income statement or balance sheet.

**Convenience level.**

Do not buy it if a stock will keep you up at night for any reason. This guideline uses even if the capital escalates or if all your friends fill up on the hot name. No investment, even a profitable one, makes good sense for an investor who can't buy into the idea with the shares.

Question # 6: How do I identify when to trade a stock?

Answer: Whole books have also been composed on this topic. Because they only buy stocks they like, most investors find the sell choice harder than the buy decision. As soon as you purchase a stock, you take pleasure in owning; you may find it difficult to do away with the investment.

That said, there is nothing like a permanent buy. Eventually, every stock outlasts its energy in your portfolio. All stocks move up and down with time, but the unsightly plunge of bank stocks in late 2008 and 2009-- far worse than the drop in the broad market-- highlights the risks of sticking with stocks when their environment changes substantially.

Rudiments of the Stock Market

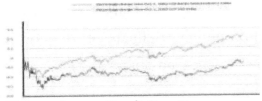

Figure above - Don't Buy It

1) If you bought the capital because of its appraisal, does the valuation still look appealing? If growth drew you in, has that development continued? Consider selling if the response is no.

The business has radically changed. Often that drug company you acquired because of its pipeline of asthma drugs changes its instructions and starts to concentrate on mental-health treatments. Do not be scared to sell if you like the first method, but not the second.

In late 2007 and early 2008, when some enemies started grousing about banks overstretching themselves, lots of financiers bailed out on their stocks. Financiers who heard the train coming and sold their paper stocks in 2004 and their bank stocks in 2007 benefited from their ability to see and from their willingness to accept the new reality.

31

Question # 7: My stock has dropped, but I can't find any news on it. What triggered the dip? Answer: You might not know. First, you should recognize that the stock market reflects the collective will and viewpoints of millions of financiers. If enough of them choose to sell Acme Widget-- no matter their factors-- the shares will decrease in value.

In some cases, people sell a stock because it has yielded well, and they want to schedule some profits. Since shares have begun to fall and they fear further declines, stockholders might also sell. In some cases, problems from another business in the market will trigger stock to decline because the reasons behind the weakness in the other stock might affect the first stock.

And sometimes stocks sell in compassion-- perhaps when a close competitor has taken a substantial loss-- even when the news does not impact them directly; in such cases, they often rebound quickly.

Often stock will increase or decrease not because of any company-specific news but because the market itself has taken a turn. Keep in mind that stocks tend to move in a pack. As with any bag, you'll see bold names that bolt to the front while plenty of laggers hang back. If you have stocks, you should expect them to decline when the broader market declines.

Expect the broad stock market dips 10% for some months. History recommends that it could still decline even more, but ultimately most stocks will recover. They constantly do. If your capital falls 10% in a prevalent market decline of 10% without giving any unfavorable news, you can blame the broad market for the decrease.

Question # 8: How do I trail my portfolio?

Answer: Twenty years ago, most big papers printed everyday stock prices, and investors followed their financial investments in the article. With the proliferation of sites using the same information in a more modern style, often at no charge, many papers have avoided the stock pages. These days, the Internet merely uses more info, and many commercial websites do an excellent task of stocking pricing and trading data.

You can have a look at the efficiency of your stocks on your discount broker's site. While each broker does little task differently, they ought to show you the value of your stock positions and allow you to see the stocks' history-- how they have moved considering that you bought them.

Use a third-party site to track all your investments at the same time if you do not buy all your investments through the same broker. Simply input your stocks' ticker symbols, and you can have a portfolio of the stocks you own in addition to stocks you want to view.

Interested in more detail than today's share cost? You can likewise get on the date you purchased the stock along with the purchase cost and the variety of stocks. If you input your transaction details, the website you selected will show you the profits of each stock considering that you bought it-- essential information for assessing your portfolio.

Question # 9: Should I register for a newsletter or go to a broker for help about picking stocks? Or am I much better off making my own investment decisions and not paying for guidance?

Answer: The response to this question depends upon the answer to two other concerns. How much time will you commit to dealing with your financial investments? And how comfortable do you feel evaluating numbers?

People who claim to have discovered the single technique of making money in the stock market shoot emails all over. Even if a financier makes a 932% return on a stock once, you can't assume he'll do it once again.

Real stock analysis-- the kind of research carried out by experts who handle other people's money and can get fired if they mess up-- takes some time. You don't need to spend 40 hours a week, but unless you know you'll invest at least three hours a week learning about your investment, following market news, and comparing one stock with another, do not try to do it alone. Find somebody you trust-- a newsletter editor, a monetary organizer, or an online master who gives suggestions without spitting through the computer screen-- and pay attention. You do not need to follow anybody's tips precisely. Still, you'll make much better choices when you can begin your analysis by examining the stocks other people like, or when you can use somebody else's strategy to check your own decisions.

Now, about the numbers. More mathematics geeks regulate the universe. Stock analysis is not rocket science, and you don't need a Ph.D. in data or mathematics to analyze stocks. The job simply requires a versatile mind, a desire to learn a few originalities, and a calculator.

Question # 10: The stock market is dropping, but I like the Acme Widget. Should I get the shares now or wait till the price dips further?

Answer: Plenty of investors buy and sell choices based on a stock's price action-- a process known as a practical analysis.

Practical analysis looks at a stock's price chart and conclude where it will go based on where it has been. Some people make cash by doing this, and some lose it. Even professionals will concur that forecasting and timing short-term stock or market motions are very tough.

This book gives you the tools to examine stocks from an essential perspective: by looking at their operating data or appraisal ratios. You take a threat by not acquiring it instantly as soon as you get a stock with strong investment potential at its current rate. Sure, the stock might dip, providing you an opportunity to snap it up at a bargain. However, the price might also increase, eating away some of your possible earnings. As a practical matter, financiers who enjoyed a stock at $50 per share tend to discover it more difficult to shoot on the purchase after it jumps to $60, even if it increases on relevant news, and the future still looks intense.

Markets often shift direction unpredictably, and just because stocks have declined over the last week does not mean they'll keep decreasing anymore than it implies they'll reverse course. You simply can not predict. Unless you have some personal perception about the direction of the stock or the market in the coming days, don't hold back on your purchase in the hopes of purchasing a better cost.

After buying, the market could always go up or go down. Do not kick yourself for acting too quickly if the demand decreases and do not pat yourself on the back since you purchased before an upturn. If you bought the best stock, you'd enjoy your reward in time, regardless of what the market does after you make your transaction

## Why Invest?

Everyone invests. From the smart stockbroker on Wall Street to the assembly line employee who avoids breakfast every Friday because he runs out of cash before his next income, everyone invests their time, effort, and attention in what they find valuable.

You're investing in your health if you spend your Saturdays' training for a marathon or tackling 50-mile bike trips. If you spend your weekends with family activities, taking the kids to swimming practice or attending Little League video games or checking out museums, you're buying your kids. And if you go to classes in hopes that a college degree will assist you in getting a better job, you're purchasing your career.

While each of these types of investing appears to support different objectives, all of them-- and dozens more-- share a common purpose: to provide for the future. Investing in your family now can develop relationships that will sustain in times when you might need more from others yet have less to give in return.

Many people enjoy the wealthiest rewards from their investments after retirement, but the earlier you start preparing, the better you will be in the future. Making a little dedication to different kinds of investing-- the monetary strategies presented in this book-- can put you on your journey to a longer and more influential retirement.

## Common Motivations.

Motivations behind financial investing are almost as many as investors themselves. Naturally, your concerns may vary from your neighbor's, however for the many parts, motivations for investing tend to fall into three classifications:

-Investing in build wealth.

-Investing to support a family.

-Investing in preparation for retirement.

Financiers concentrated on building wealth, i.e. tend to focus more on the future than other financiers. Wealth makes you to establish and maintain a comfortable lifestyle. For some, that comfort might imply a nice-sized house, a couple of reliable vehicles, and a journey to somewhere warm for a week every January. Numerous investors are more than happy with such a lifestyle, while others set loftier objectives. By building wealth gradually-- the safest and best way to do it-- you can enhance your way of life along with your net worth.

Financiers who focus on supporting a family frequently seek to build sufficient wealth now to pay for a property in a community with good schools, the periodic trip, and things like ballet slippers, algebra tutoring, and summer season. You know the type-- the type that works hard for 40 years, climbing up the business ladder. The supreme goal for these investors is a smooth transition to retirement, where even without an income, they can maintain the standard of living they invested all those years making.

Whether you seek to support a healthy lifestyle, buy a happy home for your children, or just buy enough and keep so you will not have to work till you turn 80, you can enhance the chances of reaching your objectives by putting your money to work. Whether you're 20, 40, or 60, you'll like more options decades from now if you invest wisely-- starting today.

People who keep investing until it's hassle-free spend their golden years consuming ramen noodles. You've got to start today.

Uncertain how to continue?

Do not panic. After reading this book, you'll know all your monetary goals and some tools needed to reach them. The primary step is to avoid making a foolish-- but frighteningly common mistake.

## Don't Kid Yourself.

Lots of expert financiers-- even some who have accumulated millions of dollars in assets-- don't comprehend what is affordable to expect from their investments. All too often, they state things like, "I want yearly returns of about 20%. Greed, wrong choices, and stubbornness have torpedoed many financiers, but the most considerable difficulty inactive investing may be unreasonable expectations.

Over the last eighty-seven years, big-company stocks have balanced annual returns of 11.8%. Long-lasting government bonds returned an average of 6.1% a year given that 1926, while

Treasury expenses-- about the lowest-risk investment readily available-- handled just 3.6% returns. Small business stocks published higher highs and lower lows than large companies and bonds, and they were also more likely than big stocks to see returns vary considerably from year to year.

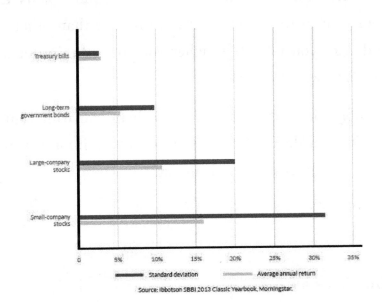

Source: Ibbotson SBBI 2013 Classic Yearbook, Morningstar.

Figure above - Stocks Outperform Bonds.

If you wish to become an active investor, commit this idea to memory:

" High threat, high return. Low threat, low return.".

Like many essential realities, the investment mantra above is easy to comprehend; but, not always easy to actualize—still, the relationship between return and risk is the foundation of capitalizing.

Every investment has its ups and downs; nothing plans a straight course. However, some paths are rockier than others. The more danger you take, the higher your opportunity for a high return-- or a significant loss.

You've probably found the wrong man to help you with your investments if a stockbroker or financial consultant informs you he can make high returns with little threat.

## Set Attainable Goals.

Now that you know the importance of investing and the different kinds of returns a few of the most common financial investments grow; it's time to proceed to your circumstance. Every person has various investment needs and strictures. No investment strategy, no matter how wise or well-considered, applies to everybody. To tailor your financial plan, ask yourself the following questions:

What are my goals? Be specific. "Get rich" will not cut it. Your objectives must set specific targets, such as, "Retire with $1 million in assets.".

What time do I need to reach those objectives? A forty-year-old mother with a daughter who will begin school in ten years must go for an investment that diff from a forty-year-old with no children who won't touch her finances till she retires at 65.

Some financiers can tolerate more risk than others. None of the approaches is right or wrong, but you'll sleep much better if you customize your investment technique to your personal feelings about risk.

What must I do to fulfill those objectives? Now you've attained the million-dollar question. Even if you set uncertain goals, you won't reach them overnight. As Table 1.3 shows, the time it needs to feather your nest depends on how quickly your financial investments grow. Split 72 by an investment's rate of return, and you know approximately for how long it will need to double your money. Earn 4% a year, and your salary increases in 18 years. An 8% return doubles the cash in 9 years while making 12% reduces the doubling time to 6 years.

| Investment development ratio | No of years to increase in price |
|---|---|
| 4% | 18 |
| 6% | 12 |
| 8% | 9 |
| 10% | 7 |
| 12% | 6 |

The above table;

Assuming you have $100,000 in your 401( k) plan and hope to retire in 40 years with $1 million in properties. According to the Law of seventy-two, if you grow a portfolio that yields six percent in a year, your account would double to $200,000 by year 12, increase to $400,000 by year 24, redouble once again to $800,000 by year 36, and leading $1 million at the end of year 40. In the nick of time to satisfy your objective.

You can't ensure yourself a 6% return. And in some cases, even if you do manage a 6% annual return, you'll sustain a lot of twists and turns along the method-- a 30% profit this year, a 15% loss next year, then a flat year followed by an 8% gain.

Taking the natural unpredictability of investing into account, you must overengineer your investment portfolio. In other words, if you want to build up a particular quantity by a specific time, plan as if you need, state, 20% more than your target. Many of all, keep those targets affordable.

For example, a 30-year-old with no cost savings and a job paying $40,000 each year who desires to retire a millionaire at age 65 should not need much risk to reach that objective. A 40-year-old with no cost savings and a task paying $40,000 annually who wishes to retire a millionaire at age 65 will just have the ability to obtain that goal if she wants to handle some threat. A 50-

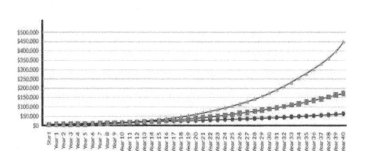

Year-old with two children, no savings, and a task paying $40,000 annually who likewise wishes to spend for his child's' college educations without loaning and then retire a millionaire at 65, merely do not have an affordable objective.

At this moment, you may be asking, "How can I know whether my goal is affordable?" The figure below ought to help.

The Power of Time.

Too frequently, investors concentrate on the gulf between what they have and what they end up being and want to be discouraged. Do not fall under that trap, since you have not embarked on this investment journey alone. You have a capable ally: time.

The image shows the power of time on investment. If you invest at the rate of 7.5% annually, $10,000 will increase to more than $20,000 in 10 years, and then to $42,000 in 20 years. After 40 years, that $10,000 will have turned into a $180,000 nest egg.

Investments seem to grow quicker in later years because of the results of intensifying. The investment showed in the image never really accelerates its growth on a portion basis, but as the numbers get bigger, the nest egg appears to grow faster. Suppose you invest $10,000 and make a 10% profit. In the last month of the year, you have a rate of $11,000. If you repeat the 10% return in the second year, you'll acquire not only another $1,000 but an extra $100-- the 10% return on the $1,000 you gained in 2015. With time, the excess return made on previous gains will enhance your portfolio's value significantly.

Don't panic. People with 40 years to invest enjoy many options. And while financiers with much shorter time horizons may have fewer choices, this book can help you make the best decisions possible.

# CHAPTER TWO

## Myths and Misconception about Stock Investment

There are some myths and misinterpretations about investing in stocks. To have a more understanding of what it truly means to be a stock financier, be sure that you understand the truth behind the misconceptions: Investing in Stocks is Having a bet

This is why people run away from the stock market. Take note that the costs of stocks in the market depend on particular variables, such as the economic climate, organization performance, customer habits, and technical advancements, among others. The costs of stocks do not rise and fall arbitrarily.

Whether the securities market is betting or otherwise depends on how you approach it; if you merely pick the stocks randomly and simply depend on pure luck to be successful, after that, you are gambling. You can expect the same effects as you would definitely when you wager in the online casino. Nevertheless, if you come close to the stock market expertly where you place a short time, effort, and research, in all your transaction, if you take into consideration every act as an investment choice, then you are not wagering yet investing. Gamblers depend on luck, while real investors understand what they are doing and have a side over the stock exchange.

Buying Stocks will undoubtedly make you a Multi-Millionaire Investing in stocks is similar to any type of different other business: You can make money; nevertheless, you can also shed money. Like any investment, there are risks involved. Indeed, some of those can grow their cash, but many financiers lose their money. To be successful, you need to know the stock exchange and apply particular methods. Indeed, a significant component of success is to carry out a considerable research study.

It is worth noting that you will just gain a specific portion of your financial investment. Naturally, you may earn more than 100% or perhaps 200% of your investment. Do not expect it to happen overnight. For that reason, the more cash you spend, the more income you can make.

If you are in a particular exclusive group, the Stock Market is Only for the Rich People Some assume that you can only invest in stocks. This is not true. The securities market is open to every person given you are of age, and there are no other legal prohibitions relevant to you in your state. Especially today where you can buy stocks by just opening an account with an internet broker, you can invest despite only $300, or perhaps much less.

## You Need Connections to Succeed

With all the links that Warren Buffet has, there is no surprise he can determine the appropriate stocks to spend in. Well, if this is what you believe, then you are wrong, absolutely incorrect. Yes, having great connections can help you leverage and also increase your possibilities of choosing the right stocks and also earn a profit, but handling the stock exchange is more than building links. In truth, several investors make appropriate amounts of income even without connection with anyone whatsoever. Many thanks to the Internet, which essentially makes our world smaller, you can quickly access different sites and also gather details from the convenience of your house. There are also many evaluations and evaluations shared by other financiers that you can use as an additional recommendation. Here is the reality: You do not require links.

## Duration.

What you need is to find the securities market and deal with your winning approaches.

## You need Extensive Financial Knowledge

This is one more myth that needs to be broken. Indeed, having financial knowledge is something that you require to help you to pick the most active stocks to purchase. This is real, mainly if you use financial analysis-- which is one of the most typical investing strategies. There are various other approaches that you can use without you having to look at any number. This, naturally, does not mean that you need not to bother establishing your financial understanding. However, it just shows that you can still make and spend cash by buying stocks, even if you have minimal expertise in business finance. It needs to remember that you do

You can establish your financial expertise just by researching stuff online. The crucial part below is to analyze what you currently know.

Quick way to earn money

If you have significant funding and also can deal with many shares, then you can earn money by buying stocks rapidly. However, just some people have the true blessing of having millions or billions of funds in their checking account. Likewise, if you are a beginner, the best way is to begin small no matter how much capital you have.

## An Easy Way to earn money

Considering that you just have to pick stocks and also invest in some cash, wait for some time, and after that market to enjoy your earnings, after that generating income with the securities market must be very easy, best? I am afraid that is a No. You can do all these with merely a few clicks of a mouse, investing in stocks is not as straightforward as it looks. The main problem hinges on selecting the best stocks to purchase, in addition to the appropriate timing. Now, for you to recognize these two significant points, you need to apply severe initiative and also the time in research and analysis.

Your Partners in Crime; For best stock trading experience

Before you can spend in the stock market, you need to open an account with a broker. The issue is, with all the brokers out there convincing you to sanction and make a financial investment, how do you identify the broker that can suit your requirements? Make sure that your broker passes this type so that you will certainly have the ideal investing or stock trading experience.

## Banking

This is a fundamental part to consider before you even transfer any money right into your account. Make sure to inspect the down payment methods, in addition to the approaches for making a withdrawal. It is not unusual to locate brokers that use even more alternatives when making a deposit but just have limited choices for making a withdrawal. You would certainly not wish to have your cash locked up in your account with no way to withdraw it right into real money.

A broker will typically ask you to submit a copy of your identification papers before it also processes your withdrawal. Before you make a down payment, see to it that you recognize what these papers are, which you have them in your belongings. Otherwise, you may not be able to withdraw your cash.

## Minimum Deposit and Withdrawal Limit

Take note of the minimum down payment calls for. Some brokers need a minimum down payment of a minimum of $250, while others may approve a small amount of just $25. You should be aware of the minimum and maximum withdrawal limits. A broker may also bill a low withdrawal cost, which is normal. If you mean to make several withdrawals in a week, after that, the withdrawal charge is something that you must pay attention to.

## Demonstration Account

Your broker ought to give you a free demonstration account. This is an excellent means to get a feel of real trading in a real-time stock market setting without running at lost.

## Costs

These fees usually are just a tiny amount, they can quickly load up swiftly, mainly if you make huge sales in a short period. Be sure to contrast the different brokers that you locate online and look for the one that stocks the least expensive fees.

## Trading Platform

Every online broker will certainly give you an investment platform where you can buy and sell stocks with just a click of a mouse. Your broker must give you an expertly created platform with useful attributes. The best brokers will offer you cost-free information or details concerning the securities market to help you make the best financial investment decision. Your broker also needs to provide you with charts and even graphs in case you intend to make use of technical analysis.

## Trading Restrictions

Some brokers will also put a constraint as to the number of stocks that you can sell or buy.

You need to only work with a broker that will allow you to invest on your own.

It also needs to permit you to trade as many stocks as you want.

Before you also sign up for an account with any kind of broker, be sure to examine the testimonials given by various other financiers. A secure way to do this is to use your favorite internet browser to search for the name of the broker and add the word testimonials. It is not scarce for brokers to employ freelance writers to come up with a positive review of the broker's organization.

Pay attention to the time when the latest testimonials were done. If the most current favorable evaluations were made about a year ago after that beware. After all, the management group and also the policy of a broker might change periodically.

## Mobile Feature

These days, people access the Internet using their cellphones. It is less complicated and more convenient. Your broker should also give you a platform that has a mobile feature. This implies that you need to have the ability to manage your account and make investments by only using your mobile phone, and also, the procedure must be as convenient as you are when you use a desktop. Do not fret; brokers with a high score always have a mobile feature. Having a mobile feature is among the reasons people like specific brokers.

## Customer Support

Remember how you can call the customer assistance group. Exists a number that you can call any time? Also, inspect if the broker provides a live conversation feature on the website. If the broker can only be contacted through email after that, evaluate how fast it can respond, and focus on exactly how specialist it handles your inquiry. When you make your first withdrawal, an excellent way to do this is by sending a message to client assistance asking for any kind of alternative documents that you might send requests. Ideally, the consumer support should be able to respond with an answer to your query within 24 hours.

# CHAPTER THREE

## What to Do to Be a Successful Stock Investor

Using strategies alone is insufficient. To also boost your opportunities of earning a profit, you need to observe the best techniques complied with by capable stock capitalists.

### Sufficient Research

It is not shocking why so many people lose their cash when they purchase stocks. Although books on the subject always stress the relevance of doing findings, just a few can research appropriately. Regrettably, many financiers assume that only because they have investigated the market for two hours, then it would be enough to come up with a sound financial investment choice. This is wrong. Make sure that you do adequate research. A research study should be an all-natural component of your day-to-day life if you are serious about a successful financier.

## Start Small

It doesn't mean the amount you have in your account that you want to invest in. It means that you first use a demonstration account so that you can examine the water without running the risk of any cash.

Always start small. Your objective is to acquaint on your own with the real technique of trading stocks, also, to create a winning strategy. Do not worry; when you have a reliable approach in place, you can always enhance the quantity of your financial investment, which will also improve your possible profit.

## Diversification

Expanding your investment is just one of the best means to minimize your losses. As they say, you must not place all your eggs in one basket. The factor is that no matter how a lot you examine the securities market, it can just boost our possibilities of success. It can never ensure the return of positive earnings. The fact is, there is a possibility that you might also lose your financial investment. Investing in stocks has its threats, just like any various other rewarding financial investment possibilities.

By expanding your financial investment, you can reduce your danger and minimize your losses.

The most common means is to purchase stocks from different companies and not put all your money into a single business. An industry that is blossoming today might no longer be considered a rewarding financial investment tomorrow. Spread your financial investment over different markets.

Possession class diversity is an additional means to branch out. You do this by buying the various property class, such as in bonds, products, others, and stocks. You must discover how to time it well when you apply this approach. For instance, in the situation of economic healing, shares may be your best asset to buy. In an example of recession, investing in bonds might be a much better option than investing in stocks. Technique diversification is an additional efficient way to lower your risk. Depending on where you wish to spend or how you want to invest (short-term or long-term), particular approaches may be more relevant than others. In an instance of a lasting financial investment, you can not disregard the use of business evaluation.

When it comes to a temporary financial investment, technical analysis might be one of the very best approaches that you can use. You may also make use of geographical diversity. Some capitalists are quite partial and purchase a business that lies in a specific territory. Remember that no industry in a particular geographic location can outmatch others continuously—Ups and downs are standard in the securities market. You can also expand regarding time. Remember that you do not need to invest all the cash in your account in one trade. You can scatter your investments over time. For example, you can spend 20% of your money today and then follow it up with 30% in the following month. Much like anything in the company, proper timing is vital to success.

Diversifying simply means spreading your financial investment and not placing it in a single basket. Bear in mind that branching out alone is not a trick to revenue. One vital part of expanding is choosing where to diversify and place your money. Consequently, you can not sacrifice the value of studying and analysis.

## Avoid complying with Expert Advice at all times

When you are a novice, you may find it handy to search the web for pieces of advice coming from the supposed "specialists." This is a standard error because not all of these "professionals" are actual professionals. These days, it is reasonably straightforward to spread a word and advertise one's self online. If you are good at advertising, you can quickly project an image that you are a professional stock financier of which you have not invested in any stock before. It is also worth noting that even the real experts commit blunders from time to time.

The best way to avoid depending on experts is to create your understanding of the stock market. What separates an expert from a complete novice is that an expert has his very own view of the stock market and can sustain his sight with sensible defenses. At the same time, a beginner generally counts on what other people say.

Beware of the Pump and Dump Scheme

A business or somebody that possesses stocks advertises his stocks and spread favorable reports about them. When this takes place, other investors will use to acquire the shares, assuming that they are a significant financial investment. The result is that the seller of the stocks makes a revenue, while the purchaser has a stock whose price is frantically dropping down.

Remember that the pump and dump scheme is not a bad thing. You can gain from it and earn an income.

The secret is to purchase the stocks before or quickly after the preliminary part of the pump and dispose of the scheme. The right way to do this is to sell the shares after you small amount of revenue. Don't wait for the increase to stop.

## Do Not Hold the Stocks for Too Long

It deserves keeping in mind that not all financiers lose their money for choosing the wrong stocks. Some lose their money because they want the right stocks yet hang on to them for too long. Do not ignore the volatility of the stock exchange. See to it to market your stocks before their price drops. Take your revenue while you still can.

## Understand Volatility

You should have a proper knowledge of what volatility is. Many people think about volatility as something where the costs of stocks merely rise and fall nearly arbitrarily. They frequently believe that after a massive surge, then a considerable fall can be expected, and the other way around. This is not always the case. If it were so, then instability would be very easy to foresee. Numerous pressures influence the volatility of the stock market. This means that even after a substantial decrease in the costs of stocks, it is still possible that a further decline will occur. This likewise implies that the outcome of a specific trade depends on previous sales or purchases. Regrettably, some people believe that given that their last three financial investments did not work out, after that, it is most likely that the next trade will bring profit with a positive result as long as they use the same approach. This is wrong.

There is an excellent chance that the succeeding trade or investment will also be a loss. The reason depends on the strategy that you are using. It is a sign that you must change or at least modify your technique if the method maintains on shedding. Real expert capitalists do not count on pure good luck. They recognize that if they come up with the right winning method, then the possibilities of raking in some earnings would be high. Keep in mind that if you have the right approach, there is still a possibility that you might shed an investment. No strategy can guarantee 100% the return of favorable revenues. However, with consistent research, hard work, and technique, you can turn a favorable outcome to your side and develop a winning edge over the stock exchange.

## Maintain a Trading Journal

Even though it's not called for, keeping a trading journal can be useful. Don't worry; you do not have to be a professional writer to maintain a trading journal. Nevertheless, you need two things:

One, you need to be completely sincere.

This means that you must admit and accept your difficulties and weaknesses, in addition to the result of every financial investment that you make with no bias.

And two, you need to upgrade your journal regularly.

Preferably, you should write in your journal the reasons why you want to invest in stocks, and your short-term and also long-term goals. Your journal should likewise include your techniques, the financial investments that you make, and even your objectives.

It will make it much easier for you to detect any weak point or component of your method that still requires to be changed. Again, the essential thing is for you to be straightforward with every detail that you compose in your journal, and also update it regularly.

## Do Not Approach Investing as a Hobby

The depressing fact is that many people who purchase stocks approach the securities market as a hobby. Although you are always totally free to consider it a simple pastime, you can also anticipate getting a fair result equally as when you come close to any different other services as a mere leisure activity, with no dedication. You need to take it as a business or an occupation if you want to get the right quantity of regular earnings from your investment. The issue with those that consider this type of investment as a mere pastime is that they fail putting in the right initiative and findings that will enable them to increase their possibilities of making a profit.

## Wait it Out

Occasionally the best method to deal with the stock exchange is simply to wait it out. When the market is merely going down, it is unavoidable that you will soon come across a time. As opposed to being too worried and putting speculative financial investments, simply wait it out. Waiting investment out does not mean that you would neglect the market. It means that you ought to follow what is happening in the market, yet do not make any kind of move or financial investment. Wait for the best time to act. When the market recovers, then make sure that you want to make the most of it.

## Do Not be an Emotional Trader

When you invest, it isn't enough that you feel good and also make regarding it. Instead, you need to be confident of your investment since you have done the right study and research, and that are good reasons to believe that it is the best financial investment. Anytime you feel like your feeling is getting in the way of your decision making, quit, and don't spend in any kind of investment whatsoever.

## Capitalize on a Bull Market

An advancing market describes the securities market. It indicates that the prices of the stock on the market are rising-- which is good. On the other hand, when the prices are falling, it is called a bear or bearish market.

You should know how to make use of a bull market. Of program, the key right here is to be able to acknowledge that a bull market in the present situation of the market or when a proceeding market is just about to take place. You need to place your settings (financial investments) as early as possible to make sure that you can capitalize on the increase in the prices of stocks. A bull market usually occurs after a bearish market. You must know as soon as possible when a bear market would end, and a booming market would start. To do this, you have to meet up with your day-to-day study and valuation. A decree market may be promoted on the news; the best way to take advantage of it is by placing your financial investments at its creation. The factor is that an advancing market is usually complied with by a bearish market. It may currently be too late for you if you wait for a bull market to be introduced before you act up. Take note that the means to be in advance of the securities market is to be ahead of the competitors. Be the first to get hold of every possibility.

## Examination and Develop your Strategy

Always evaluate your approach and also examine it several times before you use it with actual cash entailed. If you just change a minor part of your technique, take note that you have to repeat this process. The best way to do this is by using a demonstration account or by investing the minimum amount.

Remember that as a beginner, your primary objective is not to gain money right away. When it comes to success in the stock market, the more knowledge you have, the more your possibilities of hitting the appropriate financial investment. It takes time to know the best investment choice.

## Never chase after your Losses

This is a general advice offered to speculators: Do not chase your losses. A fantastic reality about this is that lots of people who run after their losses are well aware of this advice. Despite the understanding that it is not a good idea to run after one's injuries, they still fall into this mistake.

So that you will not lose control of yourself, make sure you have the strength to stop making any kind of financial investment when you come across a considerable loss. Give yourself time to forget everything concerning the stock market. People generally chase after their losses by placing a more substantial investment with the hope that they will recover what they have lost and have more profit. After all, they have currently spent some time and initiative. The secret below is that rather of chasing what you have already lost, you should be composed and focus on your winnings or income. Bear in mind that every investment that you make is one-of-a-kind from all the remainder. When you run into a loss, simply admit and approve the damage, and move on. After all, the best strategy in the world will lose from time to time. Once you add up every little thing, the vital thing is for you to end up with a positive profit.

## Only Invest the Money that you can Lose

Another standard rule given to casino players is to only play with the cash that you can lose. Well, although you will certainly not be gambling, you have to understand that this is still an investment. And, like any other type of investment, there is an opportunity that you may not make any profit or even lose all your cash.

## Do Not Be Tired

The great stock investors have their own unpleasant stories to tell. They have experience of being overwhelmed in the stock market. As you go and spend more time investing in stocks, you will also encounter countless challenges.

## Relax

Give yourself a break. It is so straightforward to obtain addicted to the stock exchange, especially when you realize some profit. But you have to give yourself time to relax. If you bear in mind that you can come up with much better financial investment decisions, allow your soul to rest. Likewise, it requires time to make a substantial profit in the stock market. As a result, give yourself time to loosen up every time, and afterward come back to work more durable.

## An Overview of Different Strategies

You can not have a constant stream of income by investing in stocks unless you have a reliable approach. You are not limited to using one strategy. You can combine the policies, modify them, and come up with your plan. The important thing is that you make use of an approach to transform the odd in your favor.

## Fundamental Analysis

Anybody who has invested in stocks or any business has probably experienced this method. This is one of the most common and practical strategies that you can use. Fundamental analysis emphasizes on the basics of the company concerned. After all, the performance of stocks in the market only depends on the performance of the business. Hence, this strategy involves examining the cash flow and financial statements of companies. To a certain degree, this strategy also considers the quality of the company. But, the main focus of this strategy lies in the performance of stocks in the market, which depends on the efficiency of the company. When you use this strategy, your goal must not be simply to gain from the capital gains but to receive all the advantages of possessing a prosperous company.

## Practical Analysis

This strategy deals with analyzing graphs and charts, which show just how the rates of stocks change within a specific time. It is believed that many variables that affect the performance of stocks have their accumulated effect on the scale.

When you use this strategy, the secret is to seek a pattern or trend. You must then benefit from this pattern. Take note, nevertheless, that models come and go

Sometimes you may not see some pattern at all. A common blunder committed by many investors is that they force a design. Don't look for a pattern if it is not visible.

## Value Investing

This method has to do with buying a company that is presently trading below its real worth. As an example, if the actual cost of the stocks of Company A is $25 per stock, but the stock exchange only reveals that its stocks are just worth $15, after that, it has to be a profitable investment. The trick here is to be able to take the evaluation and benefit from it.

When using this strategy, you need to look for stocks that have solid basics. If the true worth of a stock is $25, but it is rated at $15; after that, its actual rate will soon increase.

Remember that when you use this approach, you do not only look for a stock that is selling at a low rate. If the stock of Company A uses to sell at $23 per stock, however then they now go down to $14 per stock, it does not mean that they are good stocks to invest in.

## Development Investing

This technique was accepted in the 1990s, when industrial firms were on the increase. At that time, several financiers who used this technique were able to obtain a considerable profits. It is to be noted that this approach is riskier than other methods.

The best means to know this strategy is to compare it with worth investing. This is the reason why a growth capitalist might buy a stock that is presently trading higher than its actual worth.

Again, a great investor looks into the future to see if a particular stock will be selling at a higher rate in the future, after that, the investment that you make today can be taken into consideration a successful one.

When you make use of development investing, the best stocks to buy are those that have a high capacity to grow. Growth financiers pay close attention to new and little business. This is because small and largescale enterprises have immense potential and space for development.

## Qualitative Analysis

This approach provides a vital focus on the high quality of a company. It also takes into consideration the management approach of the company or the style by which the people of the firm mean to achieve its objectives. Appropriately, there is an excellent opportunity that the rate of its stocks will increase, which makes it a good investment.

## Stock Split Advantage

A company usually proclaims a stock split when the price of its stock gets too high that is no longer eye-catching to investors. When the rate of capital is too expensive, it tends to project a picture that it has currently reached its top and makes people think that the stocks are no longer an excellent financial investment.

So, how does a stock split work? If you have thirty stocks at $20 each and a stock split is announced, then you will be with sixty stocks at $10 each. It is a fair division. The stocks will increase after the split, yet their rate will also decrease. It worth noting that a stock split is not limited to dividing a stock into two. A stock split might divide a stock into three or more divides

How to use this strategy is to check out a business that has simply declared a stock split. The stocks of that company might be an excellent investment if the stock split was legally done due to a growing investment. Naturally, you ought to also discover as high as you can about a company and also make your analysis. Counting on a stock split alone is not a good idea.

You need to understand the inverse split. The reverse split is also known as stock split but in the opposite. Compare to a stock split, and a reverse split is not a good sign. Keep in mind to run away from a company that uses a reverse split.

Right here is exactly how the reverse split works: if you have ten shares of stock at $10 each in Company X and a reverse split is performed, after that, you will have five shares at $20 each. As you can see, the cost of the stocks has increased significantly. A firm might make use of a reverse split to tempt investors to make a financial investment. As you can see, it is a deceitful relocation. The boost in the cost of stocks is not caused by any kind of progress or growth in the company but only by simple control. Indeed, a company that exercises a reverse split may be successful in the future. Such an act is a sign that the company is already having a hard time at present.

## Revenue Investing

Take note that when you spend in stocks, you come to be a part-owner of company service. When you use this method, look for a huge and well-established company that no longer look for expansion. Instead of using the investor's profits for the growth of the company, these companies pass dividends to investors.

An important thing to note is that when you gain income from dividends is that in most states, such earnings that you receive from revenues are taxed at the same rate as wages. You can anticipate a higher tax than the ones enforced on capital gains. Check the regulations of your state to have more knowledge about the tax regulations that might be suitable for you.

## Stock Mastery

You can adapt this strategy for a long time. How this works is that you need to pick a specific stock or company, and you need to learn about it every day until you have a perfect knowledge of how that stockwork. Remember that the more you know something about a stock, the far better you will be able to predict its actions-- and this is the key to incomes.

## Can Slim

Can slim is an acronym that means Current quarterly incomes, Annual revenues growth, new products, services, management, or high rate, demand and stock, Leader or Laggard, Institutional sponsorship, and Market direction? According to this technique, by just looking at these factors, you can determine the best stocks to purchase.

How do you use this method?

The first step is to identify the stocks that have a quarterly revenues increase price of at ] at least 25%. Because you also need to be particular with the growth of the company for the long term, you need to even think about the development of the annual income of the company. This technique means that you ought to search for a business that has 25% yearly revenue growth (minimum) for the past five years. You need to also watch out for companies that stock something new to the market. Researches show that out of the typical characteristics of the best stock performers is that their firms have something new to stock to the market. You must also bear in mind the rule of stock and demand. If a minimal item has a high requirement, then the effect is that its price will rise. In a company, this rule of stock and demand is always present.

The next thing that you need to determine is the origin of the stocks. Does the company known as a leader in the industry or a laggard?

Of course, your purpose is to obtain your stocks from a leader. When you use this strategy, only receive your stocks from reputable companies. Many activities in the stock market also come from mutual funds and pensions, so also watch institutional sponsorship.

## Buy and Hold

This is the usual means of buying stocks. It is thought that although it is challenging to say the instructions of the stocks market for a short-term period, you can expect the costs of the stocks to increase in the long run. Since everybody in the stock market intends for those instructions, this is. Therefore, it is said that so you can hang on high stock for a more extended period, then you can enjoy profit in years to come.

This is the expected outcome bearing in mind that an investment society is included. Remember that you will be holding the stocks for a more extended period; after that, it means that you will not always be investing.

Therefore, you will have lower costs and taxes to worry about.

# CHAPTER FOUR

## How to Buy Your First Stock?

Buying stock is not such as getting much else. When you go to the book shop and purchase a book, there are some threats. When you are buying stocks, you usually pay a great deal even more than what it would set you back to purchase a book, and also the danger of losing it is also more higher.

Before you start buying stocks, you need to know 100% of what you are doing. I would recommend you set up a brokerage firm account now so that it's ready when you're ready, but make sure you do your finding and also shops around there.

First, learn about stocks. Learn what they are, how they work, how they give you money, and how to know them.

Stocks aren't complicated, yet they aren't easy. They will take a little time to figure out, and you will need to understand how they work.

How can you earn money from something if you do not know how it works.

You can start choosing and researching companies as soon as you know the system. Look at different markets. For adequate diversification, you have to ensure you possess stocks in various industries. When you knowhow the sectors you choose affect each other and also work with each other, and as soon as you have them chosen, explore different company, you have an interest in. Look for companies you know and understand. You do not have to buy from them for them to be good stocks. Take a look at companies that you have seen development in and see a great future with.

When you've selected some stocks, research them. If they do not look good, do not buy the stock.

You need to be all ready before you buy your first stock. You can start investing in stocks.

Purchasing Your First Stocks Can Be Confusing
People who don't understand much about the stock exchange commonly search for information online. They browse for things like "stocks for novices" because they feel overwhelmed and confused before they start. If you do not know the stock market,

the excellent point is that you don't have any money in it and also have not lost anything this last year. Now, anybody that has money in stocks possibly feels sick right now because of how much they have lost.

You need to gain from this horrible market change that absolutely nothing is risk-free in the stock market. Some people have shed a lot more than they should have because they were overconfident and had most of their income in stocks. Also, some lost because they had too much in one specific stock or one particular sector.

When you spend in the stock market, you should always acquire a range of stocks. When you buy stocks that are in different sectors, you make sure that you will not shed every little thing if one of those markets happens under challenging times.

Today the securities market means down from its highs some years earlier. A ton of money has been lost, along with lots of people's retirement cost savings. If you are in the stock market, it must feel like your pocket has been selected. The issue all of us face is that at some factor, the market will reverse the program, and many people will not have anything to return in to make some of the lost. Currently, it looks like the market will not go up, yet it will, and you have to be ready. If you have nothing left from now fiasco, nonetheless, there will be nothing you can do to reclaim some of your losses.

Buying Your First Stock - Hints, And Tips For Those New To The Market

The stock market is an exciting place. If you're thinking about entering it, you're probably excited about the possibility of making some money.

Before you purchase, do your study. I can not worry about this enough. There are lots of professionals available who can give you handy advice. Still, there are also many people out there that believe they are professionals, and their information may not be as reliable as you think. If a friend gives you advice and also urges you to buy because such a company is warm, make sure you didn't follow their guidance.

I would recommend any beginner to start with stable stock. Select a company that has been around for a long time and research them. Financial publications are practical, as are sites such as Reuters. Look at how the business of your choice is doing, and what the state of the market look like in general. This will assist you in making your choice.

The reason for choosing a company and stock that has been around for a while is because you'll be much more likely to forecast what will certainly occur in the future. New companies might be superb to buy, and we are all aware of how people can make a grand revenue out of them, but the threat of losing your cash is substantial.

For that reason, the more strong stock could not offer a great deal of excitement, buy it can give a bit of satisfaction while you discover what's acquaint on your own with the world of finance and stock profession. There is a lot to learn, and this takes some time.

The stock market is affected by so many outside influences, including lawful events. The tort system has had a significant impact on the market in the past, and huge decisions are collective.

Another piece of recommendation is to start small while you are finding out. It real that the securities market can be seen as a little bit of a wager, and there is always a certain quantity of threat included. Absolutely nothing is inevitable, but you can reduce the risk of monetary loss by doing your study and by maintaining a close eye on the influences that could influence your stock.

## How to Prepare for Your First Stock Market Trade

Action 1: Set Up an Account with a Broker

If you're planning to make your professions, your best option is to opt for a discount broker online. They are much more affordable than complete brokers because they don't offer you all the new services like financial investment advice and various other services you probably don't need. If you're making your stock decisions, you should simply pay for the profession.

If you want to be a short-term trader, also known as a day investor, look for a website that gives affordable professions if you trade frequently. Look for a broker that specializes in providing cost-effective long-term professional charges if you want to invest for the long-term.

Action 2: Learn the Ropes

You can miss this step if you're ready to trade. If you just decided you want to invest, but you don't know how to take your time on this. It is incredibly crucial to understand what you're doing, or else you'll simply be gambling.

Step 3: Set Up a Strategy and Choose your Investments

Stock investing is everything about approach, despite how simple or complicated you make your way. Use the details you discovered from step 2 to set up your strategy—use the guidance from successful financiers like Warren Buffett to construct a method that will work.

Bear in mind that regardless of how excellent your technique is, there will always be a risk. Because one stock choice was terrible doesn't mean you're a terrible investor and must give up. Just put yourself together, change your method as possible, and move on.

Step 4: Money

Place money aside to invest. It's vital to invest in the stock market because, without it, you won't have the ability to purchase any type of financial investment. Start saving your income as soon as possible and be adding money to your portfolio on a routine basis.

Step 5: Buy

The last action is to acquire stocks and also get going. You made your options, currently go to your broker agent account, and make your professions.

A First Lesson in Learning How to Trade Stocks

For anyone learning how to trade stocks, it is essential to know the difference between investing and trading in the securities market.

The discussion here is directed not to the investor but to the neophyte investor, a person who has yet to discover how to trade stocks, one who is thinking about putting their cash at risk. A risk that can be lessened by complying with some useful standards rules pointed out but disregarded in the excitement, success, failure, or greed, that the present sector of stocks market exhibit.

The trader is typically more active than a financier in acquiring and marketing stocks, holding the stock settings for a shorter period in the attempt to make gains when they occur or to lessen the inevitable loss that belongs to speculative trading.

Yes, substantial profits can be made when investing in the stock exchange, to the extent that somebody can be financially independent.

It takes time and initiative to discover the principles of stock trading and determination to follow reasonable standards to handle risks and make the needed action in those standards. When encountered with the demand to act, to offer a losing placement, the lure is to simply wait for a little while, "perhaps it will recover" is the thought that supersedes the rule that brings about"sell!".

When they are wrong and allowing revenues to run when they are right, great investors take high-risk examining by limiting losses.

There are many reasons stocks change in price at the time, and it is the goal of the investor to buy or sell stocks and benefit from those changes to purchase stocks at a lower cost from which they will rise or sell stocks at a rate where they will fall. This way, when transactions have been completed, if an expected total revenue has been achieved, a receipt a minimum of close or equivalent to the expected target profit, it can be taken into consideration that the purpose has been met.

No formula can guarantee revenue, and successful investors approve the reality that they will indeed make unprofitable and profitable investments. The requirement, regarding possible, is to reduce the losses and to optimize the gains to make sure that the overall outcome will be rewarding to the level that the return on the capitals at risk will be more than if they were used to purchase another investment.

## Buying Stocks - Making It a Smart Financial Move

Joining the stock market can be a smooth economic action. The different factors you ought to discover about previously making this financial step is how the stock market works, the ups and downs of the stock market, knowing what to buy and how much to buy, understanding when to buy and when to sell, and many more.

Investing in stocks can be a very profitable business if you learn all of this before you sign up with the stock market or the stock exchange. This is the reason why investing your cash generally is a good idea. There is the potential for high returns to any kind of investment. Stocks are not the only things that people can purchase. People can buy companies, personal home mortgages, property, and many more. Nevertheless, among the most popular investing strategies includes stocks.

Purchasing stocks can be so profitable that many people make earning from it. They make their cash by buying and selling stocks. One way to maximize your gain in a stock profession is buying many shares of a stock when it has reduced and afterward selling all the stocks as quickly as it increases in worth. When you buy the stock when the price is low, then you reduce your risk as well because the loss will not be significant in that situation.

You should also have the ability to forecast how well the stock will perform. Your opportunities for losing money will increase if you buy a stock that is predicted to execute poorly. On the other hand, you may obtain a stock that increases in worth; in that case, you stand to gain a significant amount of money. An investing consulting company focusing on the stock exchange can guide you on which stocks to buy. It is also a good idea when purchasing stocks to spend in a sector that you have experience with. By doing this, your wishes about buying a stock or selling your stocks are more probable to be correct.

**Stock investment Tip**

Do this: put your money in a stock, then for the rest of the year, don't look at your account or learn what's happening in the stock market. What do you think your report will look like after the years?

Do you think you'll be a millionaire?

Below's what's going to happen.

If you are lucky, you'll have some gains. You'll lose most of your cash if you run into bad luck.

"Take or leave it" method is no different than betting. Throughout a year, a whole lot of things can happen that will affect the stock you own. You have to take note of these things, or you might regret it.

Despite winning stocks, they claim their breakthroughs are short term. The significant gains in these uncommon stocks will last from one to three years. Like all other stocks, they decline and also are no longer attractive to buyers that wanted it.

On the other hand, a champion stock will give you many chances to contribute to your position and produce better gains. If you practice the "set it and neglect it" approach and did not pay attention, you would have missed an opportunity to pyramid your setting.

Simply look at how many people lost in the recent stock market crash. You would have found out near the leading and gotten back in near the base that generated lately if you pay attention to the markets.

Buying stocks isn't an easy search. If we want to minimize our losses and optimize our gains, it calls for energetic engagement and taking decisive action.

# CHAPTER FIVE

## Mechanics of OwingStock; How to Choose a Stock Broker

You've done the tricky part. Picking stocks-- without a doubt, is one of the essential products of the equity-investing process-- requires more time, initiative, and belief than any other parts of the task. But your responsibilities don't end there. They didn't even start with stock selection.

It is assuming stock picking as choosing a path to the journey of financial liberty, understanding, of training course, that the course will frequently change to accommodate the detours and weather condition risks that are market instabilities.

In this session, you'll learn how to choose a broker, how to buy and sell stocks with that broker, and how to limit your tax obligation. Consider it a quick glimpse of this book. Pay attention to the journey. With some patience and persistence, you'll get where you want to go.

## Who Does Your Trading?

Have you ever asked the question, "So how can I find an excellent broker and not someone who will jet off to the Cayman Islands on my penny?" Words "broker" doesn't load people with confidence, and many people have captivated that, though, mainly because a few brokers have absconded with investors' funds. Realistically, if you make use of a traditional brokerage home, you need not bother with funding for a thief's permanent vacation.

Securities Investor Protection Corporation (SIPC) works to help investors hurt by crooked brokers, saying to have returned assets to 99% of investors qualified for defense. The SIPC doesn't help you recover your losses if you buy the wrong stocks and lose your tee shirt. Simply put, if you get scammed or suckered in a worthless investment, that's your problem. But if a broker steals your money or losses it in the process of doing something unethical or illegal, that's the SIPC's issue.

So do not lose sleep over a broker stealing your money. Instead, focus on picking the best stocks, and concentrate on what kind of broker to use.

Discount brokers, such as TD Ameritrade, E * Trade, Charles Schwab, or Scottrade, buy and sell stocks on behalf of investors at lower rates. While the four noted above represent some of the best-known price cut brokers, dozens of others give online trading services for less than $10 per deal. For the majority of investors that want to focus and pick their stocks or act on advice from a third-party specialist, such as a newsletter, a discount broker will do the trick.

**Full-service brokers.**

On top of making professions for you, full-service brokers might also give guidance or do various other solutions. If you look for stock advice or your economic circumstance requires customized help, a full-service broker might make good sense. Be ready to pay more for your professions-- in some instances $50 per deal or more.

To compare brokers, just visit their internet sites and sneak around. Processing stock purchases have come to be an asset company, meaning that all the companies do it well. When you study brokers, try to find features relevant to you, such as:

**-Minimum account dimension.**

Many brokers sales price cuts for accounts over $25,000 or $100,000, but low rollers don't get specialized treatment, and all brokers need minimum balances of accounts. If you are ready to start small, make sure your broker can accommodate you. Minimum account sizes usually differ.

**-Web site style.**

Each broker website features its interface. You'll find some even more intuitive than others, and the ones you choose might not attract another person. When it comes to navigating a broker's site, rest lesson suggestions from others and more on your own

**-choice.**

Quantity discount rates. If you wish to make a lot of investment (as a beginner, you should not), some brokers lower their fees for regular traders.

**-Range of safeties.**

All brokers sell stocks and ETFs. If you intend to purchase standard mutual funds, look around. Some brokers stock a multitude of shared funds available for a no-deal cost, but the choice and rates differ significantly from company to company.

**-Research study solutions.**

Some price cut brokers provide access to online devices, stock screeners, and research records. Some allow clients to interact in online neighborhoods where investors share ideas.

If you 'd rather stay away from brokers entirely, you can buy stocks directly from the company that provided them (or directly from the transfer agent the company hires).

Dividend reinvestment plans (DRIPs) permit capitalists to buy stocks without a broker. Many of the strategies state that you must already possess at least one share of stock in your name before you can participate. DRIPs do not bill brokerage commissions, but the majority of them examine small charges for buying and selling shares.

Alternately, when you purchase stock with a broker, it certainly belongs to you. Because the broker has custodianship of the shares, they are held in the broker agent firm's name-- usually referred to as the road name-- for easy buying, selling, and transferring. Instead of allowing the broker to use its road name, you can pay to sign up the shares in your name and have the physical certificate sent to you.

Investors like DRIPs because they allow the reinvestment of money dividends in company shares, also if the payments are smaller than the share rate. For instance, if your holdings in a stock trading at $50 per share pay a $5 dividend, you can buy and reinvest the reward 0.1 shares of the stock. Many DRIPs also allow you to add money to the account in percentages-- sometimes as low as $10 a month.

The ability to slowly add money to multiple stocks with time interest investors who do not have much money but who plan to allot cash for investment regularly

DRIPs bring in investors that want to develop a wide range gradually and that don't plan to trade often. Because many small stocks and big ones don't provide the plans, DRIP financiers appreciate fewer choices for numerous investors; 1,000 shares still look like many choices.

How to Trade Your Stocks

Essentially, beginners ought to deal with their stocks at the original price.

Before you make a transaction online, see your broker's web site and click the trading link. The site will ask you the number of shares you want to buy, and whether you wish to make a market order or a limit order.

The broker will make the deal at the best available cost when you place in a market order to buy fifty shares of Acme Widget. If you've examined Acme Widget and like the stock at $40 per share, it shouldn't matter the price whether you buy at $39 or $41.

Limit orders, on the other hand, are for investors who want to buy or sell only if the share price reaches a certain degree. For instance, if you take into consideration Acme as being expensive at $40 yet would acquire it at $35, you can submit a limit order with a $35 rate, and the broker will buy the shares if they dip to $35 or below. Restriction orders give higher control over the price paid for a stock, yet they can keep investors out of stock. If

Acme goes down to $35.01, then climbs to $50, the financier with the $35 limit order will not purchase the stock and share in the gains.

Investors also use restriction orders on the sell-side to secure gains. Intend Acme trades for $40 per share, yet you would certainly such as to sell and book your revenues if the rate rises to $45. A limitation order to offer at $45 will get you out of stock at a price not less than $45, as long as the stock climbs to the target degree before the order runs out. Brokers usually charge higher compensations on limit orders than on market orders.

## Reading a Stock Quote

When you open a financial web site and enter your ticker, you'll see a web page with some numbers. While each website makes its pages in different ways, you can trust seeing the majority of this info:

-Inquire rate: The lowest price a seller is ready to accept for a stock. For most huge, heavily traded stocks, the bid and ask price will be close with each other. For sparsely traded stocks, the bid-ask spread can be vast.

-Quote cost: The highest possible cost a customer agrees to pay for a stock. At any given time, brokers handle countless deal orders, a few of which means a particular charge to sell or buy a stock.

-Present rate: This number reflects one of the most recent deal prices, though free websites normally run on a delay, so their names are a bit obsoleted.

Day's range: The low and high rates in the current day's trading.

Fifty-two-week range: The high and low prices over the last year.

Volume: The number of shares traded.

Last, note that if you access a quote web page after the market closes, you'll see end-of-day numbers. You'll see intraday numbers if you go during trading hours.

Some investors like to make use of stop orders-order that turn into market orders after the stock hits a limit. If the shares rise and fall below $35, the stop order starts, and your broker sells the stock at the prevailing cost.

Regrettably, stop orders have limitations. You'll sell at around that price if negative news breaks, and the stock instantly dips to $30 per share. A sell limitation order will not assure you a sale at $35, just that you'll market the shares at the going rate once the cost dips below $35.

Investors who make use of stop orders likewise run the risk of buying or selling stocks simply because of the market relocations. Suppose you set a stop order at 10% below the stock's present rate to safeguard against hideous losses because you are afraid the company will lose a patent lawsuit that might cost millions of dollars in sales. What happens if the market falls 15% and your stock slides with the rest of them? No trial has surfaced, and the reasons you bought the stock is still intact. Yet the stop order would have sold you out of stock, which probably stands a high chance of recovering when the marked retrieves its momentum.

In short, limits orders allow you to get into stocks if they fall or get out of stocks if they rise. Stop orders will enable you to get out of stocks if they fall or get into stocks if they increase.

Your broker will give you many trading options beyond the market, limit, and stop orders. As you gain experience, feel free to expand your horizons and try new ways to trade. But anything you do, no matter your investment goals, don't forget the most critical trading rule: If you don't know how the trade works and why it makes sense, don't make the trade.

Come to think of it, that rule applies to many aspects of investments.

## Limit Your Taxes

Only a fool makes financial investment decisions without considering the tax implications. On the flip side of that coin, only a fool allows tax obligation problems to be the principal driver of those same decisions. Because they don't want to pay tax obligations on the profits, many investors decline to market stocks at a revenue. But when the situation changes, and it no makes sense to hold the stock, failure to sell might cost them.

The good news is, managing tax obligations on your financial investments is more annoying than it is hard. With that in mind, below are three questions about taxes that every investor needs to be able to address.

> First Question: How much will I pay in taxes when I collect rewards or sell my stock?

Answer: Because Congress can change tax rates, this question has no permanent solution. According to tax obligation prices that took effect at the beginning of 2013:

Many stock returns and bond rates of interest settlements will be exhausted at the taxpayer's average earnings price.

Temporary capital gains (profits on the sale of stock or other securities) will be strained at the average income price. You owe tax obligations at the short-term rate if you sell a possession after holding it for one year or less.

Long-term resources gains will be taxed at 0%, 15%, or 20%, depending on the investor's income.

As always, you only accumulate tax responsibility when you sell your shares. If you buy stock for $1,000 and it skyrockets to $10,000 in a year, as long as you hold it as stock, you don't owe a dollar of tax obligations on it.

> ➤ Second Question: How can I protect my investments from tax obligation liability?

Answer: personal retired life accounts (IRAs) allow financiers to postpone taxes on investment proceeds. Some salesmen sell IRAs as if a unique company can set them up, and after that, direct financiers to companies that charge huge fees to handle the accounts. That's not how IRAs work. IRA can be set at any type of brokerage, and you can buy stocks, bonds, mutual funds, and other monetary properties within an IRA.

Recently, financiers under age 50 can add a maximum of $5,500 to their IRA; payment restrictions have increased over time, and this trend is likely to continue. You can deduct contributions to an IRA from this year's taxes.

However, if you or a partner contributes to another retirement plan through a job, you probably can't. And you can only add to an IRA if you or your partner earns taxable income.

Investors can start taking cash out of their IRAs at age 59 1/2, and they need to start after they turn 70 1/2. IRA circulations undergo government earnings tax, and also, if you get rid of cash from an IRA before the age of 59 1/2, you'll owe federal income tax obligation plus an extra 10% charge.

A special kind of IRA-- the Roth IRA-- enables investors to grow their money tax-free. Roth IRAs need some hurdles. You can't deduct the contributions, your income and tax-filing status might limit how much you can contribute.

> Third Question: My job offers a 401(k) retirement plan. Should I sign up for it?

Answer: Almost definitely yes. As long as the strategy gives you the investment alternatives that do not stink, the advantages of a 401(k) are too appealing to neglect.

The 401(k) strategy allows your employer to deduct a portion of your salary before taxes and spend it-- usually in mutual funds-- and some employers will match your payment to a particular degree. The business could match 50% of your contribution to 6% of your income.

While your contributions, your company's contributions, and any type of dividends and also gains in the portfolio are not subject to income tax obligation promptly, similar to IRAs, you'll pay tax obligations when you withdraw the funds-- after retirement.

# CHAPTER SIX

## Building your Perfect Portfolio

Since you have a sense of the power and significance of diversity, it's time to create your target profile. While this book can provide you with a structure, no formula or cookie-cutter technique will churn out the best possession allotment for each financier. To do this right, you'll need to make a couple of judgment calls. Start by asking yourself the following four questions.

### 1. How much Do You Need?

Investors can make several sorts of errors as they prepare for the future. But perhaps the most usual-- and the most harmful-- is not understanding how much you need.

IS $1million enough? That depends on when you retire, how long you live, and how much you want to invest. Check the following table, assuming you manage to sock away $1 million by the time you retire, and after that, spend enough to gain 5% per year after inflation.

| Portfolio at retirement | $1,000,000 | $1,000,000 | $1,000,000 |
|---|---|---|---|
| Annual living expenses, rising 3% per year with inflation | $120,000 | $100,000 | $80,000 |
| Year 1 | $930,000 | $950,000 | $990,000 |
| Year 2 | $856,500 | $897,500 | $979,500 |
| Year 3 | $779,825 | $842,375 | $968,475 |
| Year 4 | $698,291 | $784,494 | $956,899 |
| Year 5 | $613,206 | $723,718 | $944,744 |
| Year 6 | $523,866 | $659,904 | $931,981 |
| Year 7 | $430,059 | $592,900 | $918,580 |
| Year 8 | $331,562 | $522,545 | $904,509 |
| Year 9 | $228,140 | $448,672 | $889,734 |
| Year 10 | $119,548 | $371,105 | $874,221 |
| Year 11 | $5,525 | $289,661 | $857,932 |
| Year 12 | $0 | $204,144 | $840,829 |
| Year 13 | | $114,351 | $822,870 |
| Year 14 | | $20,068 | $804,014 |
| Year 15 | | $0 | $784,214 |
| Year 16 | | | $763,425 |
| Year 17 | | | $741,596 |
| Year 18 | | | $718,676 |
| Year 19 | | | $694,610 |
| Year 20 | | | $669,340 |

The table - Living off $1 Million

Somehow $1 million doesn't look like a tremendous amount after you crunch the numbers.

If you plan to amass a $1 million after retirement, and after that live on $120,000 a year each year after you retire, you would be ready to work until you're 75-- or die reasonably young. (For the document, the retired person who can live on $60,000 a year and sustain a 5% financial investment return after inflation might extend his $1 million for 36 years.).

## 2. When Will You Need the cash?

This question has a straightforward answer if you do not plan to touch your financial investments until retired life. On the other hand, if you need $100,000 for college expenses in 10 years, or if you want to buy a holiday habitation years before you retire, now is the time to make it up. As a general policy, the shorter the financial investment time, the lesser you can depend on stocks, which tend to be unpredictable.

Between 1926 and 2012, there have been 66 periods of 20 years-- 1926 through 1946, 1927 through 1947, and so on. Neither stocks nor bonds have ever posted a decline for20 years. Large-company stocks lose worth in just 4 of the 78 periods of 10 years, while neither corporate neither government bonds ever had a negative return. When it comes to five-year periods, the image changes substantially. Large-company stocks decreased in 12 of the 83 five-year periods, or roughly 14% of the time. Long-term corporate bonds declined in just 3 of the five-year periods, and it hasn't taken place in more than 40 years.

Keeping primarily stocks in the profile makes sense if you're looking 20 years out. You possibly need some extra bond exposure if you're going to need the cash in five years or less.

### 3. How Much Can You Invest?

The answer to this question depends on two things: how much you realize, and how much you spend to live. You have more control over the second than the first.

When it comes to this question, you have to be sincere. Who doesn't think he's worth $100,000 per year? But, most Americans won't smell that annual salary.

You can build up a nest egg even if you don't make $100,000 per year. Don't believe it? The table below demonstrates how swiftly you can develop a financial investment portfolio.

|  | $100 per month | $200 per month | $500 per month | $1,000 per month |
|---|---|---|---|---|
| Year 1 | $1,200 | $2,400 | $6,000 | $12,000 |
| Year 2 | $2,496 | $4,992 | $12,480 | $24,960 |
| Year 3 | $3,896 | $7,791 | $19,478 | $38,957 |
| Year 4 | $5,407 | $10,815 | $27,037 | $54,073 |
| Year 5 | $7,040 | $14,080 | $35,200 | $70,399 |
| Year 6 | $8,803 | $17,606 | $44,016 | $88,031 |
| Year 7 | $10,707 | $21,415 | $53,537 | $107,074 |
| Year 8 | $12,764 | $25,528 | $63,820 | $127,640 |
| Year 9 | $14,985 | $29,970 | $74,925 | $149,851 |
| Year 10 | $17,384 | $34,768 | $86,919 | $173,839 |
| Year 11 | $19,975 | $39,949 | $99,873 | $199,746 |
| Year 12 | $22,773 | $45,545 | $113,863 | $227,726 |
| Year 13 | $25,794 | $51,589 | $128,972 | $257,944 |
| Year 14 | $29,058 | $58,116 | $145,290 | $290,579 |
| Year 15 | $32,583 | $65,165 | $162,913 | $325,825 |
| Year 16 | $36,389 | $72,778 | $181,946 | $363,891 |
| Year 17 | $40,500 | $81,001 | $202,501 | $405,003 |
| Year 18 | $44,940 | $89,881 | $224,701 | $449,403 |
| Year 19 | $49,736 | $99,471 | $248,678 | $497,355 |
| Year 20 | $54,914 | $109,829 | $274,572 | $549,144 |
| Year 21 | $60,508 | $121,015 | $302,538 | $605,075 |
| Year 22 | $66,548 | $133,096 | $332,741 | $665,481 |
| Year 23 | $73,072 | $146,144 | $365,360 | $730,720 |
| Year 24 | $80,118 | $160,235 | $400,589 | $801,177 |
| Year 25 | $87,727 | $175,454 | $438,636 | $877,271 |
| Year 26 | $95,945 | $191,891 | $479,726 | $959,453 |
| Year 27 | $104,821 | $209,642 | $524,105 | $1,048,209 |
| Year 28 | $114,407 | $228,813 | $572,033 | $1,144,066 |
| Year 29 | $124,759 | $249,518 | $623,796 | $1,247,591 |
| Year 30 | $135,940 | $271,880 | $679,699 | $1,359,399 |

The Above Table - Building Wealth a Month at a Time.

These are not wrong numbers, and they assume you never get a raise-- and hence never enhance your month-to-month financial investment. The more you can save, the extra you'll have when you need it. And also herein lies one of the most vital keys to developing wealth: Spend less than you make.

Despite what your investments do from year to year-- and you definitely can't trust them delivering such stable development-- if you invest less than you make every year, you'll have enough to support on your own and set some aside.

## 4. How many risks Can You Handle?

Some investors need a 10% yearly return to meet their monetary goals. That's a high obstacle. People have handled it, however accomplishing 10yearly returns over a long time would exhaust both the ability and the good luck of many expert financiers, not to mention that of beginners. What happens if the kind of securities required to make a run at 10% annual returns will keep you up in the night? You have two options:

a. Live in anxiety. (This is not ideal.).

b. Alter your purposes so you can meet your goals with a less risky profile.

Many people select option one, but option two makes the most sense, both for your portfolio and your nerves.

In the most investment business, fear of unpredictability is called risk hostility. The term applies to fear of investment decreases or volatility. Everybody worries about losing all their money, but that isn't the issue below. Stocks are likely to give exceptional returns over a 20-year duration, but you can't sit in your rocking chair and wait 20 years. Purchasing the stock market entails dealing with the movements of your stocks day-to-day and year-to-year. This's where risk hostility can be found. Everybody has some level of risk aversion. The higher your degree of risk hostility (the better your fear of loss), the less risk you can tolerate.

Your degree of riches also influences your risk tolerance. If you have $1 million in the bank, make a great living, and also won't require your financial investments for 20 years, you can pay to take even more risks than somebody with $10,000 in the financial institution.

## Running the Numbers

You'll better comprehend what you need from your profile when you address the four essential concerns. And with that knowledge comes power.

Questions one and two-- how much money do you need, and when do you need it-- will help you identify your needed price of return. The list below formula will give you a rate of return for any starting and ending factor, assuming you want to grow a basket of cash and don't want to add any kind of new funds:

( What you require What you have) ^ (1 Year till you need it)-- 1

If you need $1 million, and you have $100,000, and you plan to retire in 25 years, it looks like this:

($ 1,000,000 $100,000) ^ (1 25)-- 1 = 0.096 = 9.6%.

What if you have nothing, yet you can devote funds to invest over time? You can quickly produce a table like the wealth-building one earlier to plot different situations. Here's the formula:

[Portfolio value X (1 + Rate of return)] + Annual financial investment = Portfolio value a year later.

The following is an example of the beginning of a wealth-building table, starting with the following assumptions:

Begin at the end of the first year, putting a year of investment contributions in your brokerage firm account.

You contribute $500 monthly.

Your investments grow at 8% a year.

Year 1: $6,000.

Year 2: $6,000 X (1.08) + $6,000 = $12,480.

Year 3: $12,480 X (1.08) + $6,000 = $19,478.

Construct that formula in a spreadsheet, and you can see the length of time it will take to reach your objective. Alternatively, if you recognize when you need to achieve that objective, try different prices to determine the kind of the returns required to get you there at the right time.

Before you move on to the last action, ensure you've avoided these four pitfalls:

- Unreasonable expectations.

If your required rate of return is more than 10%, change your presumptions. Even 10% of profits will be adamant, and any type of plan based on the possibility that you can gain more than 10% will fail extra frequently than it does well. Don't kid yourself. Ensure that your investing estimates reflect inflation.

- Neglecting expenses

Try to add extra amounts to your budget. You may be ill. Your house could refute. Your brother-in-law may guilt-trip you to backing his restaurant, even though you understand most restaurants fail. Life happens, and things that cost money are part of life.

- Underestimating your needs and lifetime

Plan for $70,000 if you think you'll require $60,000 a year. Plan for 25 if you think you'll live 20 years before retirement. The more traditional your estimates, the most likely your investment plan will accomplish its objectives.

- Deciding

OK, now, you have an idea of what you desire and the type of returns that are wanted to get you there.

That leaves just one question: What goes into the profile?

At this moment, go back to the rule of thumb that you need to deduct your age from 110 and put that portion in stocks, and after that build from there:

Are you ready? If so, add 5% to 10% to the stock allowance, depending on how comfortable you are with your level of riches.

How's your risk resistance? Add or subtract as much as 10% from the stock allowance, depending on your strength for danger. Risk-takers add to the allocation, risk-avoiders deduct.

When do you need the cash? If your time perspective is greater than 15 years, amount to 10% to the stock allotment. If you want to use the money in less than ten years, subtract 10%.

While previous instances have used average returns for quality, below, you have to depend on annualized returns. And over the long haul, large-company stocks have taken care of annualized returns of about 10%, long-term government bonds of over 6%, and Treasury expenses about 3.5%.

Why Use Annualized Returns?

Annualized returns assume stable development without any variants, and also they will certainly always lag the average annual performance. In actual life, investment returns differ from year to year, and the better the variance, the higher the difference between annualized and ordinary returns. For example:

The perfect world. Invest $100 at 10% this year and next year, and you'll have $121 at the end of two years. That's a two-year annualized return of 10% and an average return of 10%.

Messy fact. Spend $100 at an unfavorable 20% this year and a favorable 51% following year, and you'll have $121. That's a two-year annualized return of 10%, but an average return of more than 15%. A return of negative 35% for the first year and a positive 86% for the second year gets you to $121, but with an ordinary yearly return of more than 25%.

Annualized returns to say a more accurate story. Because approximating the variance in yearly returns over long periods is impossible, the majority of long-term projections assume annualized returns.

While it takes a lot of effort to compute annualized profile returns, those three historic returns allow you to approximate the yearly returns using large-company stocks, long-term government bonds, and short-term government bonds. The target annualized return of your profile is 8.8%.

Here's how to get there:

**Equation.**

( Stock allowance X Stock returns) + (Bond allocation X Bond return) (70% X 10%) + (30% X 6%) = 7.0% + 1.8% = 8.8%.

Remember, this is just an approximate portfolio return based on approximated stock and bond returns. It's a work in progress-- and at best a rough estimate-- today you have enough to contrast your expected return (the performance you require to obtain where you wish to go) and your target return (the yield implied by your target allocation). If your needs exceed your target, you'll either have to tackle more risk-- as in selecting a higher stock appropriation-- or scale back on your financial investment targets.

No one likes to reduce their objectives or realize they can't indulge throughout retirement. It's better to make an effort to discover how far your resources can take you. After that, you can change your objectives to match your fact.

Life is great if your target exceeds your requirements. You can reduce your danger to boost your possibility of accomplishing your goals, or you can try to construct a new wide range-- potentially providing increased flexibility in the future.

## Closing It Out.

Whew. It took some work, but by now you should have a good idea about how to reach your financial location without running out of cash. After you understand the principles in this book, take the campaign to increase your understanding of investing. It's not far too late to begin working toward your objectives for the future, and despite how you learn, you'll not figure everything out.

The trip never finishes. Thankfully, the techniques in this book must get you off to a great beginning.

# CHAPTER SEVEN

## How to Minimize Losses and Maximize Gains with Stocks?

When it comes to money, what matters most is not how much you earn, but how well you handle what you have. Being able to enhance the cash you have considered is the hallmark of real money management, and also one of the most efficient ways to accomplish this is to invest in stocks. Market researchers assert that for five years, buying stocks can produce, at a minimum, a 20% return.

To earn money by investing in stocks, an individual should first know the rules of trading. These rules are mandatory and are regulated to secure both financiers and the trading industry itself. Considering that somebody can face prosecution for bending or damaging these policies, investors might find it helpful to find out more about the regulations on the specified website to have more understanding.

There are two primary means you can buy stocks.

The first is investing, which is where a specific search for long-term gains in the stocks market, and purchases companies that offer potentially higher growth. This strategy calls for in-depth research of firms to determine the best ones to invest in, yet brings relatively little risk. The downside is that not everybody has the time or the ability to recognize all the financial details of a company.

One style is called trading, which is where the investor tries to benefit from the ups and downs of the stock market. The success of this approach will depend partly on the personality of the investor, as the short-term volatility of the stock market can be stressful. While this design of trading can stock considerable returns in a short space of time, it's not for the fainthearted.

Before investing, think of a strategy that includes plainly defined objectives, creates a personal risk profile, and establishes a long-time for investing. Knowing when to sell is as vital as understanding when to buy. Don't to time the market, but enter it in stages, benefiting from the market volatility.

Stock market investment has some kind of fundamental threats in it; this kind of investment is one of how you can make some money. You might start to spend in stocks when you are young to be safe for risks entailed in the stock market.


Securities Market Manipulation - How To Protect Yourself
Stock exchange control is among the most significant problem in today's financial world. Despite having Obama's determined relocate to stop such acts, we need to deal with the truth. No matter how risk-free and safe we think the market is, there are always those higher up that will abuse their power and use it to their benefit.

For the amateur traders, this is somewhat frustrating. Once it starts looking stronger, hands begin reeling costs in, and by the end of the days close, the market back to where it began.

These include:

1) Spend a week examining price patterns and see when bigger great deals of volume been available during the day. This is probably the more significant players attempting their hand to trick you.

2) During the day, be careful of Amateur hr. This is the first hr of the day when the brand-new novice investors come in and coldly start buying every little thing.

3) Always scale into settings and out of positions. These will reduce loss and optimize your gains.

4) Avoid chop time. This is a quiet time in the market do not trade it. Cut time got its name in the old days by amateur investors that got their accounts cut to items when they tried to buy during lunchtime in the market.

5) Always set your stop losses in the market in case something goes wrong. Take it on the chin, get up, and you will live to fight one more day.

6) Make sure you never trade alone. Always work with investors that are better than you. This will help you become much better. With the control that takes place, you will need all eyes on you.

7) Get a mentor. Get somebody who knows the ropes to educate you about how the manipulators work their magic during the day on the stock exchange. This can save you a lot of distress, but most notably, it can conserve you from losing your account.

Leave Strategies That Lock in Profits And-Or Minimize Losses

When developing a departure technique, there are three things that we should take into consideration.

1. How long are we intending on being in this trade?

2. How much risk are we willing to take?

3. At what cost point do we want to exit?"

The answer to the first question is:

A) Set revenue targets to be hit in some months, which will certainly lessen the number of trades you make.

B) Develop tracking stop-loss factors that enable earnings to be secured periodically to limit the disadvantage capacity. Bear in mind, the primary objective of any type of trade should be to protect resources.

C) Take revenues in increments over time to minimize volatility while liquidating.

D) Allow for volatility to make sure that you maintain your trades to a minimum.

E) Create leave approaches based on essential aspects geared in the direction of the longer term. Let's claim you love the company model of ISRG, and you think the company's growth possibility to be enormous. In this situation, you may wish to hold the stock long term and create a price target based on future income development. Nevertheless, if you are in a trade temporarily, you should not bother yourself with these things because they do not matter on a short-term basis. Too many short term investors try to trade on fundamentals, and it does not make good sense to do that. Fundamentals only work in the event you wish to invest in a company as opposed to trading their stock.

F) Set near-term revenue targets that perform at favorable times to make the best use of earnings. Right here are some common implementation points:

- Pivot Points (A technical sign acquired by determining the numerical average of specific stocks high, low, and closing rates.

- Fibonacci/Gann degrees

- Trend line breaks.

The secret is to learn a system that helps you and one that creates solid stop-loss points that get rid of stocks that do not work in the right manner


## 2. How much threat are we willing to take?

This will certainly establish the size of our trade and the type of stop-loss we need to use. Those who desire less risk tend to develop tighter stops, and those who presume more risk offer the position more area to maneuver or work as they state.

It is also essential to set your stop-loss points so that they are protected from being set off by average market volatility. This can be done in several ways.

The beta indication can give you an excellent concept of how volatile the stock is relative to the market in general, but these are great for longer-term traders that can endure 10% losses. An example would certainly be if the beta is within 0 and 2; after that, you will be risk-free with a stop-loss point at 10-20% lower than where you got the stock.

### 3) Where do we desire to obtain out?

You may ask, why would you want to establish a take-profit factor or limitation order where we sell when our stock is doing well? The answer is. Ideally, we do not intend to do something like this, but there are times when it for your benefit. Lots of people are crazily connected to their placements and hold the stocks when the underlying basics or technicals of the profession have changed. The only thing excellent about a limit sell order is the reality that it takes the feeling out of the trade. It either strikes your sell restriction order, or it hits your stop-loss point, and you can deal with your service after you enter your decrees and not have to stress over how your position is doing while you are away. If you are to sell this way, your exit point must be evaluated at a critical price level such as rate resistance, trend line resistance, or other technological aspects on the chart such as particular Fibonacci levels.

Leave strategies and various other money monitoring techniques can significantly improve your trading by getting rid of emotion and reducing risk. Before you enter a trade, take into consideration the three inquiries noted above.

# CHAPTER EIGHT

## How to Start Investing in Stock at $100? Or Less

The majority of people assume that you require thousands of dollars to start investing, but that's not true. I started investing with just $100 when I began working my first job in high school (of course, top institution).

It's possible to start buying at high school, in college, or even in your 20s.

Much more something to chew on - if you spent $100 in Apple stock in 2000, it would be worth $2,300 today. Or if you invested in Amazon stock at that same time, it would be work over $1,000 today, which's if you spent $100 as soon as— assuming if you paid $100 month-to-month given that 2000? You would have over $20,000 today.

Hopefully, that's pretty motivating for you and confirms that you do not need a great deal of money to start investing. Just look into this graph:

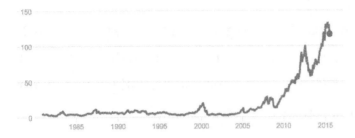

Remember, the hardest part of beginning to spend is only getting going. Since you're starting with $100 doesn't mean you need to wait, just. Begin investing now!

Allow's break down just how you can begin investing with only $100.

Where To Start Investing With Just $100.
If you want to get going investing, the first thing you have to do is open an investing account and a broker agent company. Do not allow that fear in you - brokers are just like financial institutions, except they focus on holding financial investments. We even maintain a list of the best broker agent accounts, including where to find the most affordable fees and best motivations:

143

Best Online Stock Brokers.

Given that you're just beginning with $50 or $100, you will desire to open an account with zero or reduced account minimums, and lowered costs. $0 payments, and you can invest in every little thing you wish - for free!

Remember, lots of brokers bill $5-20 to place a financial investment (called a compensation), so if you do not want an account with reduced expenses, you might see 5-20% of your first financial investment disappear to costs.

There are also other areas that you can spend on complimentary. Here's a listing of the best areas to allocate free of charge. Just keep in mind, many of these locations have "strings connected" where you have to purchase their funds or buy.

What Type Of Account Should You Open.
There are many different account types, so it truly depends on why you're investing. If you're putting your money for the long term, you need to concentrate on the pension. You need to keep your money in taxable accounts if you're investing for a shorter time.

Here's a graph to help you understand this:

**What Type Of Account To Open**

| | Medium Term | Retirement |
|---|---|---|
| Taxable | Brokerage Account | Non-Deductible IRA |
| Non-Taxable | Certain Tax-Free Mutual Funds | Traditional & Roth IRA |

TheCollegeInvestor.com

What To Invest In

$100 can expand a great deal over time, but only if you invest wisely. It's unusual to lose all your money in an investment.

To get started, you must focus on investing in a reduced expense index-focused ETF. Over time, ETFs are the least high priced means to spend in the broad stock market, and given that a lot of financiers can not beat the market, it makes sense to simulate it.

## Think About Using A Robo-Advisor

Consider using a robot-advisor like Betterment if you're still not sure about what to invest in. Improvement is an online solution that will handle all the "investing possessions" for you. All you need to do is deposit your money (and there is $0 minimum to open an account), and Betterment takes care of the rest.

When you first open an account, you respond to a collection of questions to ensure that Betterment knows more about you. It will indeed, after that, develop and keep a portfolio based on what your needs are from that questionnaire. Therefore, robots-advisor. It's like a financial advisor managing your cash, but the computer system deals with it.

There is a cost to use Betterment (and similar services). Improvement costs 0.25% of the account balance. This is less expensive than what you would pay a traditional monetary consultant, specifically if you're only getting going at $100. Practically all financial consultants would most likely pull out from assisting you with just $100.

## Alternatives to Investing In Stocks

There are options if you're not sure about getting started investing with just $100. Remember, investing just means placing your cash to help you.

Below are some of our preferred options for investing in stocks for $100.

✓ Cost Savings Account Or Money Market

-Cost savings accounts and cash market accounts are risk-free investments - they are typically guaranteed by the FDIC and are held at a financial institution.

-These accounts earn interest - so they are a financial investment. Nevertheless, that interest is less than you 'd make investing over time.

-You can't lose cash in a savings account or money market - so you have that going for you.

The most effective interest-bearing accounts gain up to 1.50% rate of interest now - which is the highest possible it has been in years!

Take a look at these cost savings accounts listed below:

## Open A New Savings Account

Another choice to investing in stocks is investing in the certification of down payment (CD). This is where you loan cash to a financial institution, and they will pay you interest for your finance. CDs differ in size from three months to ten years - and the longer you spend your cash, the higher interest you'll get.

That's a little more than their high yield financial savings account - but you have to "link" up your money for 11 months. The cool thing is that the CD is penalty-free so that you can withdraw your money any time without penalty.

Look into the list of the most effective CD prices, or compare on the table below:

-Peer To Peer LendingYou could look at being a peer-to-peer lending institution on a website like success or LendingClub if you're worried to start investing in the stock market with your $100. Peer-to-peer loaning is much like it sounds: you provide your money to others, and they pay you back with interest.

The reason why peer-to-peer borrowing is excellent for borrowers with a tiny quantity of cash is that you can separate your investment into little loans. You can lend as low as $25 per credit if you're going to start investing with $100. That means your initial $100 can be invested into four various loans. Each month these loans pay back principal and interest to you, which you can then invest right into other lendings.

With time, your first $100 might be borrowed out to multiple lendings past the first 4, and you will continue to see your growth compounded over time.

## Financial Investment Options To Avoid

There are many investments available that promote beginning investing for $5. We desire to ensure that you have a "customer beware" mindset when it comes to using these firms, and you fully know what you're entering into.

Stock Investing allows you to invest for as little as $5. However, they charge $1 per month cost on accounts of less than $5,000.

If you're only spending $5 monthly - and paying $1 in fees each month, your portfolio return is likely to suffer (or loss) money.

You'll have dedicated $60 if you just spend $5 per month for a year. However, you'll have paid $12 in fees - leaving you with $48. That's 20% of your money given up to prices.

Only in 32 of the last 100 years has the stock market returned over 20% in a given year (and that year generally complied with a bad year). The average return has been around 11%.

That's why you need to avoid services that charge you substantial costs to invest. $1 monthly could not look huge, but it is as a percentage of your $100 financial investment. That's why we like services like M1 Finance, which use commission cost-free trading without annual fees.

Simply Get Start Investing

Bear in mind, the reason that you're investing is to expand your cash over time. That means you're leveraging the power of time and compound rate of interest.

Time services your side. The earlier you begin investing, the better. Even if you only have $100 to spend, just get started.

## How to Invest $100 in the Stock Market

Investing can change your life for the better, and the earlier you start, the more you'll have in your investing account over time. Several people wrongly think that unless they have thousands of dollars in your account, there's no better area to put your cash.

The reality is that even if you only have a small amount of money, you can start investing. Consider these five perfect ways to spend a few hundred dollars. By selecting the one that attracts you based on your risk tolerance-- or by blending and matching several concepts-- you can jump on the path towards long-term economic protection and develop a nest egg that you'll have the ability to tap whenever you need it.

Five Best Ways to Invest $100.
If you've managed to save up to $100, here are our five best things to do wit:

- Start an emergency fund.

- Consider using a robot-advisor to help choose financial investments for you.

- Invest in a stock index mutual fund or exchange-traded fund.

- Find high individual stocks for your brokerage account.

- Open an IRA.


1. Start an emergency fund

It's easy to understand if your first idea was to start by taking your $100 and purchasing percentages of stock. There is much engaging evidence that investing in stocks is the best means for ordinary people to have economic self-reliance. A lot of people do not know how vital it is to have a substantial margin of safety and security with their finances. For most of us, the ideal way to have that margin of safety and security is by having cold, hard money.

If you do not have 3 to six months' worth of living expenses set apart-- possibly more if you have a mortgage and a family-- after that, the best way to start with that $100 monthly is putting it in an interest-saving account as an emergency fund.

With an emergency fund, you can not expect much of a return on your cost savings. Having that safeguard isn't about getting returns; instead, it's about keeping you from entering into financial debt or having to touch your long-term investment accounts if you have a fund emergency.

This is true if you were to lose your job or suffer an unexpected sickness or mishap that affects your income for weeks or months. Having some months of income readily available in cash will imply that life's unforeseen occasions won't affect your monetary plans. Rate of interest on savings accounts isn't high, but this is concerning securing your drawback-- not recording high returns.

2. Think about using Robo-advisor to choose financial investments for you

You're in a much better position to start investing once you have financial emergencies covered. If you like an automated method that needs as little initiative as possible, then making use of a Robo-advisor can be just what you're searching for.

Robo-advisors use apps or websites to learn more about your financial needs and, after that, come up with an investing method to fulfill them. They'll commonly use standard details like age, family risk, size, and income tolerance to design a portfolio to your demands. Robo-advisors, after that, deal with all the features of selecting investments, making sales and purchases, and keeping you informed.

The Motley Fool believes you can gain far better returns by managing your financial investments. However, numerous Robo-advisor algorithms do an excellent job, and you're likely to improve long-term results from Robo-advisors than if you never spend anything.

3. Purchase a stock index common fund or exchange-traded fund

Putting your money into a stock index common fund or an inexpensive exchange-traded fund is a great way to start investing with just a little money. Both of these investment drivers offer you diversity by allowing you to buy percentages of many different stocks with a modest investment. The general concept behind both ETFs and stock investments is to enable you to invest in the whole market or picked parts of it through a single financial investment.

You can, after that, branch out and find other investment alternatives when you've built up a strong structure in these index-tracking funds. An index-tracking fund could be all you'll need to do well with your investing.

4. Buy private stocks through a brokerage firm account

Thanks to the current approach, commission-free stock trading, buying private stocks with just $100 a month to invest is now a cost-effective choice to start investing. To begin purchasing individual stocks, you'll just need to open an investment account with a broker agent company and start making regular deposits of your $100.

Finding stocks for your portfolio can be challenging, but you can comply with some basic principles to help you get going. Primarily, don't buy any investment if you don't know its company. By sticking with acquainted firms, you'll be able to inform when they're doing well and when they're doing inadequately. Choosing a portfolio of at least 10-12 stocks will reduce the risk of significant losses if you make a poor choice with 1 or 2 of your stock choices, and avoiding stocks that make big moves in both directions is also smart when you're first getting going. Over time, you'll discover what to look for in business economic statements, and as you find out, you'll be even able to separate solid stocks from weaker ones.

Private stocks offer you an opportunity to outperform the broader market standards in the future. When you're talking about years or decades of holding high-quality stocks, the advantages of buying the best companies in the stock market can pay life-changing benefits to long-term stock investors. Also, a single share can expand all over the years to worth a considerable quantity and assist you in reaching your financial objectives.

5. Open up an IRA

Finally, the kind of account you choose to spend in can be more crucial than what you decide to buy. You should consider doing it in a tax-advantaged account like an IRA if you intend to spend $100 per month. Either a traditional or Roth IRA can offer you valuable tax obligation advantages.

Let's say that you stash $100 a month in a Roth IRA for 30 years. If you are in the 24% tax obligation bracket at retirement, having this cash in a Roth IRA can mean $43,200 in financial tax savings-- and that doesn't mean the returns and capital gains taxes you did not have to pay along the way. If you want to save more, you can put up to $6,000 into an IRA every year for 2020 and 2021 -- or up to $7,000 if you're aged 50 or more.

## Don't wait!

So if you've been holding back with your investing, don't wait any longer. Take your hundred dollars and select one or more of these five means to get started.

# CHAPTER NINE

## Turn your Stock Portfolio to a "Cash Flow Machine"

Personal finance masters are always speaking about how to come to be economically free genuinely, and you must have enough passive income to exceed your costs. That's great, yet what is passive income, and how do you get it?

In its most straightforward way, income can be broken into four groups: earned income, portfolio income, leveraged income, and passive income.

--Earned income, as you possibly figured, is income that requires you to show up to get money. Cash is earned from your time and energy. This is how lots of people make their living - as an employee.

--Portfolio income is the interest, rewards, and capital gains that originates from the possession of stocks, bonds, and shared funds.

--Leveraged income is produced when one activity earns more cash with bigger caught target markets. A speaker at a conference, for instance, may put in as much initiative to give a speech to 20 people as 1,000 people but can gain more money with the bigger team.

--Passive income is income that calls for an advance financial investment and keeps paying over and over while the needed participation wastes. The first effort creates a money machine that brings money many times over, though the participation becomes marginal.

As you can tell above, gained income only pays you what you put in. In other words, it requires your time, and you can earn raises and promotions, yet your income is restricted because there is just one of you.

With passive income, on the other hand, you can create multiple streams of income that continue to generate cash long after you did the job once. As you continue to include a growing number of cash-flowing machine, your passive income streams increase along with your wealth.

Let's consider a couple of instances so we can begin making passive income streams.

-Money Flow Positive Real Estate: Passive income can be generated from commercial or residential properties. When it comes to passive income, real estate is what many people think of. It's just passive income when the rent you receive is more than your home mortgage, taxes, upkeep, and expenditures. Or else, your rental property is simply a responsibility that costs you money - not makes you cash. You are probably speculating to make money off the appreciation.

-Certificate a Patent: Got a terrific concept or a creation? License it and make money anytime any person uses your accredited license.

-Come to be an Author: Copyrighting products that make nobilities, such as e-books or books, music or lyrics, Images, or pictures, is one more way business owners produce passive income.

-Automated Fulfillment Websites: Build an e-commerce site that can effectively process and fill up orders with little involvement to generate some passive income.

-Spend For Use Items: Vending equipment, quarter car, coin laundries, washes, video clip arcades, and storage space systems can all gain passive income.

-Build a Successful Business: A successful service in these terms means an organization that can run with or without your heavy involvement. However, for example, do you see the owner of a McDonald's franchise business on location? A franchise that is cash circulation favorable and has a team to run the market is gaining passive income;e for the proprietor.

Realize that passive income does not necessarily mean that there is no participation on your end. Producing passive income streams typically involves a substantial financial investment upfront, but in the long run, it needs little or no interaction.

Also, just because you make an earned income now (as opposed to a passive income) does not mean you should quit your day task and open a quarter car wash. To begin building passive income streams, you will likely need to keep making an earned income to convert that income into passive income by purchasing residential rental properties, and so on.

As soon as your passive income is more than your expenses, you can decide to quit making a gained income and live the rest of your life financially free.

Retirement Income Tips - Sane Strategies For an Insane Market

The excellent crash of '08 (as I like to call it) has left millions of American people and companies strapped for money. Worst but, it has left many that believed they were close to retirement scrounging to figure out what is next. A recent problem of consumer reports publication quoted a pair who summed it up when they said, "we did what everybody said we're supposed to do. It worked for a long time, but it's not working anymore."

Since we were young, the formula has been pretty clear: Save cash, diversify investments, put money in stock investments, in 40 years we will have enough to retire. Financial advisors have provided convenience through their words "over a 20-year duration the market always goes up". And worst, what happens when the market goes down, and it's time to draw out my money?

What is it "The Donald" knows that every day people do not? He recognizes what is enough to grow money. Now I'm going to share three tricks to making money in a crisis.

1) Start Buying Income Producing Assets

For too long, people have focused on buying assets that sit in an account somewhere doing very little. An example of this would be bank CDs, ultra-safe mutual funds, etc., if you desire to expand any wealth quickly, it should be placed in assets that generate income. Some examples would be a small automatic organization like a laundry floor covering or an auto laundry, if that's too expensive, consider acquiring some vending devices and positioning them in good locations. 10 Gum sphere equipment posted in the right places ought to generate about $1000/month effortless, passive income.

2) Buy Real Estate Cheap

Now that the Real Estate bubble has burst stowing away some money into an affordable residential property is a great way to create passive regular monthly cash circulation. Month-to-month rental on a residential property like this must yield $700-$ 1000/month passive cash circulation.

3) Change your stock market techniques

Sure your stock portfolio might look down, but using the leverages of options, you can rent your stock out using covered call options and make some good monthly income (Usually about 10% of your stocks value each month). Visit your broker to and how you can compose some covered calls on the stocks in your portfolio to lessen your losses.


How to Survive Today's Stock Market With Your IRA Or 401k
The stock market at its present problem is even worse than the crash of 1987 (aka "Black Monday"). The United States Secretary of Treasury, Henry Paulson, along with some government bodies, have tried to rescue the troubling stock market with

several treatments. Still, these efforts have resulted in little change.

Before we go any further on the topic of how to take control of your investments, we need to assess some standard information about"private retirement accounts" established by the government. Retirement hopefuls were able to place their IRA's and 401k's in financial investments such as shared funds, stocks, and bonds. These investments appeared to give a good range of investment choices with an excellent range of risk against tolerance and likewise used diversity to spread out the risk of investing

A lot of IRA participants know little about how to purchase these safeties because investing in the market is not precisely scientific research. You can research the business's balance sheet, anticipate what its expected possibility earnings will be, and after that, come up with a stock cost that someone may be ready to pay for in the future. I do not think that there is more than 10% of people that participate in their IRA can create this price estimate, and even if they can, there is no assurance that the company will perform to expectation, and somebody will buy that stock in the future for a higher return. That is why most people that save for retirement using an IRA or 401k do so by purchasing stock funds that rely on fund supervisors to manage the portfolio. Hopefully, these fund managers will surely outperform and get a higher return than people can do on their own. Also, these fund managers who are professionals can fail at times. On October 10, 2008, the stock industrial Dow Jones market took a 3000 point swing to the negative to a reduced of 8,300. That is a decline of about 5,700 points from the Dow Jones high of 14,000 throughout the previous year on October 10, 2007. Hedge Funds are closing left and right due to investors requesting for the investment back before suffering more looses. If professional fund managers can not give an excellent investment return to investors, how are individual investors who are saving for their retirement able to do any better?

They can do so by using a self routed IRA, which enables people to spend in a wide variety of various investment vehicles. Some of the options that retirement participants can take advantage of in a "self-directed IRA" are: accounts receivables, constructing bonds, agreements for sale, gold bullion, real estate, and of course, stocks.

Of the options offered in a self-directed IRA, stock is the option I think most financiers will know, and that is precisely what they ought to be investing in their retirement account.

# CHAPTER TEN

## How to Trade Momentum Stocks?

### What are momentum stocks?

Momentum investing is one of the hardest to define all the conventional trading approaches, but simply put, it's based on looking for companies whose stocks have been getting more potent over the previous three months to a year. The rule below is, "buy high, sell high."

### Why People ChooseMomentum Investing

Buying momentum stocks is simply a proven-effective strategy. Two people credited with identifying momentum investing, Narasimhan Jegadeesh and Sheridan Titman, showed this strategy returns average returns of 1% monthly for the three to twelve months following a given trigger occasion that signifies when to buy the stock. Their first record was released in 1993 by the American Finance Association and one more record that validated their earlier research study was published in the Journal of Finance

## The advantages of trading momentum stocks

--The first is profitability. Statistics show trading momentum stocks areas around profitable strategy provided you do your study and check your timing.

--When choosing stocks, another advantage for some is that the system doesn't need absolute precision; instead, momentum investors seek considerable incentives to take the chance of proportions. For every stock that loses a small quantity, they find at least one other several that generates a 50% or higher earnings.

--Relative simplicity is one more benefit of this approach. Many trading systems need self-control, which many people simply don't have. The method of trading momentum stocks is entirely based on accurate information that's very easy to locate, so your emotions will not take you off course.

Many people assume the turn over in this way would be extremely high, but in the majority of instances, it isn't especially poor. Frequent turning over seems to be around 90%, and while steep, it's still less than with particular other strategies.

## The downsides of trading momentum stocks

Momentum financiers do not buy stocks to hold. The stocks they hire are very unpredictable, and while the investors anticipate their momentum stocks to do well in the short-term, they're ready to sell as soon as the stock starts declining. That means if you don't get your timing right, you will not make money much.

Another complaint against the momentum trading is that economists can't seem to figure out precisely how this technique works, which makes it look like it's based on nothing but dumb luck. Some financial experts think it works because the high returns offset the risk, while others assume it's an instance of smart investors taking advantage of the mistakes of other investors, such as overreaction to hot stocks.

Many stock investors know that momentum trading can be a profitable business. You can make large amounts of money in a short period.

That's why the essential aspect of momentum trading is the understanding FILTER you employ to make your buy and sell options. There are several "superb" stock systems and trading techniques out there, yet you need to evaluate them to uncover which ones help you the more. That's part of your research as a stock trader—test, test, and test again.

The worst point that can happen to a beginner momentum investor is to get information overload. It's better to step by step and evaluate a straightforward stock trading strategy that can show you how to focus on concrete plans to generate income and pick better hot stock trading opportunities once at a time.

Fortunately, there are good sites online today that can show you how to sell a sharp and efficient means.

This momentum trading is all about trading stocks according to your expertise FILTER. You can expect to begin making a considerable amount of money regularly when you known and follow your tried and tested filter specifications like a clock.

Momentum Stock Trading - Entry Points Are Tip to Earning From Momentum Trading

Momentum stock investment is the art of taking earnings from the stock exchange with short-term professions developed to benefit from a stock's upward or downward day-to-day momentum. Lots of capitalists consider this to be a low-risk trading approach since, done correctly. With self-control, you just enter a trade when the targeted stock's momentum is already relocating in your direction.

There are a handful of crucial aspects of active momentum trading.

This book takes a look at the significance of entry points. An entrance point is a factor at which you want to enter a profession.

**Why bother setup details entry points?**

Because you want to catch the momentum once it has started, instead of buying and hoping your prediction comes true. For example, let's say Stock XYZ closed at $58, with a new hi/lo range of $55-60. Currently, you've obtained first down momentum working against you and, rather possibly, a losing trade on your hands. The trick to active trading on energy is not playing around within the new hi/lo variety.

**How do I select an entry point?**

Establishing an entry factor above the current hi (if you mean to go long) or below the current low (if you plan to go small) helps you catch bigger, much more substantial momentum in your professions. In our example, Stock XYZ was showing resistance at $60, i.e., the rate has not recently reviewed $60. I would establish an entry factor at something over $60, like claim $60.30. By setting your access factor over the most current resistance degree, your profession will only set off, given the momentum is currently entering the instructions you predicted.

If, however, there is first descending momentum, your profession will not activate, and you have protected your resources for other trades. Setting proper entrance points is, as a result, necessary to your success in momentum trading.

How to Spot the Best Momentum Stocks

The stock momentum has a high turn over rate in the past 3 to 12 months. Momentum investors typically hold a stock for a few months and check their holdings daily.

There are many stocks out there that accelerate in price and go on to make 100% to 300% returns in less than a year or perhaps in a few months.

Nevertheless, for the investors who are just beginning, momentum investing can be a confusing and discouraging experience to discover these stocks.

How to sight momentum stocks.

Among the things to find momentum, stocks are the relative stamina of the stock compared to the overall market over a given timeframe. A lot of momentum investors look at a stock that has outperformed at least 90% of all stocks over the 12 months, when significant indices decline, an excellent momentum stock exhibit strength by holding or perhaps exceeding their highs. When the significant indices rally, momentum stocks generally lead the rally and make new highs outmatching the market.

Possible momentum stocks ought to show in the equilibrium sheet that they are growing at a high up rate.

Also, a favorable forecast by at least some analysts on the Company's profits in necessary for determining momentum stocks; even more momentum financiers also check out whether the reported incomes exceeded the experts'forecasts compared to the last quarter.

A business can not expand its profits quicker than its Return on Equity, which is the Company's earnings divided by the variety of shares held by investors, without increasing money by borrowing or selling even more shares. Some companies raise money by issuing stock or loaning, yet both alternatives decrease earnings-per-share development. For momentum investors, a potential stock ought to show an ROE of 17% or far better.

-Meager trading quantities show the markets do not have an interest. Typically, momentum investors seek those with a minimum amount of 100,000 shares, or at least see their average everyday quantity increases as the value of the stock rises.

-Start keeping a list of prospective momentum stocks and track their performance out there. With time, you will have the ability to spot the stocks that go make-up to 100% to 300% returns in less than a year, or even in a few months.

Exit Strategies For Momentum Stocks

Over the last 16 months, a lot of stock markets have declined over 50%, and some private companies have been washed out thoroughly. The result of many portfolios has been devastating.

## So, how does a financier or trader know when to sell?

Well, my point of view is from someone that focuses mainly on price and volume instead of the fundamentals of the underlying business. Undoubtedly, I've had some shares that have fallen a little bit. I intended to hold them as long term investments, but it has been quite painful to watch them decline to current levels. This market has clearly shown that the buy and hold technique can devastate your portfolio if you do not make use of a form of protection, such as choices, stock index futures, and shorting strategies.

Now, back to the question of when to sell. Nevertheless, some hedge funds and Commodity Trading Advisors made a whole lot of cash recently. Some made large bank on a collapsing credit market and shorted the financial stocks. Investors that I am more familiar with having substantial success in trading in the commodity and money markets.

Generally talking, the majority of Commodity Trading Advisors (CTAs), traders that make a living by managing funds with the trading of futures markets and options on futures, can be regarded as trend followers.

Trend following investors exploits the broad patterns that happen in the financial markets from time to time. Recently, there were many significant patterns in the markets, and probably the only best trend that these investors made easy money has been in the sag in Crude Oil.

Pattern complying with traders does not try to choose bases or tops. They await a market to tell them when a design might be starting, and they will leave when the mark suggests that trend might more than. During the period where the markets are rough, these traders do not make money and tend to experience some substantial drawdowns on their equity. With the rigorous application of risk management in their portfolios, some of the far better-performing investors will reduce the volatility of their portfolios.

## So how does this apply to stocks?

Well, most people wish to be able to capture that warm stock when it moves 500% or more. The professional trader will have separated his/her feelings from the stock and left when indicators were that the trend was over.

However, there is no one specific price level, or indicator that the specialist counts to leave his setting at the same time. Instead, he will go at different cost factors within the fad.

How to identify when it is time to start taking earnings in your stock, and when to leave altogether.

Let's assume you bought shares of JRCC as it was breaking out to the upside from a small base back in April of 2008. This breakout occurred at about the $20 level. The stock then rallied over 300% in less than three months to a high close over $60. The astute investor would not have exited his entire placement at that level, considering that it is impossible to pick a top. The smart investor would have started discharging some shares around that $55 level and would have left the position between $45 and $50.

The stock had shot higher on four consecutive trading days, with a gain of over 30% during that time structure. The stock was going to the moon, and at the same, when a stock goes to the moon, it needs to come down to earth.

On June 19th, the stock opened over $2 at the open, after that shut down practically $3 for the session.

On that day, its trading range reduced considerably, as its volume, compared with previous trading days. The next day, on June 24th, the stock shut down virtually $6, and nearly 9%, its biggest down day of the trend. Traders following this stock must have left all settings by the end of trading on this day.

Currently, if you want an even more idea for leaving a high momentum stock such as this, simply go 50% of the position when it makes a ten-day lower in cost and the rest when it makes a twenty-day lower in price. This is an unemotional way of exiting a stock placement. Sometimes, you will leave a positioning way to early in a trend since stocks will trade out shorter-term investors, yet a 20 day lower is a good sign that current, intermediate-term trend is over. Longer-term investors who might make use of a methodology such as the CANSLIM technique to entre momentum stocks at 52-week highs might instead exit a position if the stock makes a ten-week low and after that a 20 week low. You will provide up considerable unrealized gains by waiting for a 20- week lower, so it is a great idea to pay attention to the cost and volume relationships talked about formerly. Or, you can leave at a five-week low and ten-week low.

These are simply some ideas on when to exit stock positions after they have made significant relocations. There is nobody perfect exit technique. If you trade in this way regularly, you will experience good profits in the long run, and you will be forced into 100% money when the market suffers the type of bear market we see now.

Momentum Stock Trading - Stop Losses Are Essential To Capital Preservation

In momentum stock trading or any other approaches of day trading, a trader requires a means to decrease the risk of losing trades. Making use of stop losses is crucial to an investor's resources conservation in that stop losses limit the size of a losing trade. A stop loss is a pre-designated price factor at which a trader chooses to exit a business with very little damage.

## Why Use Stop Losses?

There are two primary reasons to use quit losses.

-Firstly, establishing a quit loss help to manage your trading risk and maintain your capital for future trades. The reality for day traders is that not every trader is a winning trader.

-Stop losses enable a small activity in the cost going against you but cap the quantity of adverse motion you are willing to soak up. By leaving a trade that is breaking you with only a little loss, you will have protected your trading capital for future professions.

- Secondly, stop losses assist in eliminating emotional trading.

As an investor, you need to guard against being in a trade too long while wishing for a turnaround. Set correctly, your stop loss will allow for small changes in cost but protect you from more effective momentum violating you.

## How to Set an Effective Stop Loss

Let's use the following example: Assume my research reveals that Stock XYZ is poised to the run-up. It closed the previous day at $41.53, with a daily high for that day of $41.95. I generally establish an entry point at least $0.10 greater than the previous day's high, so in this situation, my access point maybe $42.05. Using a reward to take the chance of the proportion of 2:1, I would certainly put a stop loss at $41.75 and an exit price of $42.65. This trading plan stocks a prospective benefit gain of $0.60 and minimizes any loss to $0.30.

When setting stop losses, bear in mind to take into consideration a stock's current resistance levels in addition to a stock's recent trading variety.

## Tracking Stops - Adjusting Stop Losses Within a Winning Trade

Experienced day traders have found that about 1 in 10 trades surpasses expectations, i.e., the stock's momentum carries the price beyond the targeted exit price. I advise using routing stops when this happens. In the above example, let's state that Stock XYZ exceeded our assumptions, going past $42.65. In this instance, I would change my stop loss approximately $42.65 to secure in the first $0.60 of earnings and keep changing the stop loss upward in $0.10 or $0.15 increments to "trail" the higher momentum.

# CHAPTER ELEVEN

## Insider Tricks Used by Professional Traders

Insiders who sell or buy stock must submit reports that document their trading task with the Securities and Exchange Commission (SEC), which makes the records readily available to the public. You can see these records either at the SEC workplace or at the Web site of the SEC, which preserves the EDGAR (Electronic Data Gathering, Analysis, and Retrieval) data source

www.sec. Gov/Edgar. HTML

-Form 3: This form is the first statement that experts give. Experts should file Form 3 within ten days of obtaining expert status. An expert submits this record also if he hasn't purchased yet; the report establishes the expert's status.


-Form 4: Form 4 is a document that reveals the expert's activity. For instance, Form 4 would include a change in the expert's position as a shareholder-- the number of shares the person dealt with or other relevant variations. Any type of activity in a specific month should be reported on Form 4 by the 10th of the following month. If, for example, an expert markets stock throughout January, the SEC must obtain the record by February 10.

-Form 5: This yearly record covers transactions that are tiny and not needed on Form 4. Deals might consist of minor, interior transfers of stock or other arrangements.

-Form 144: This form offers as the public statement by an insider of the intention to sell a limited stock. After an insider decides to sell, he submits Form 144 and then must sell within 90 days or else submit a new Form 144. The insider must provide the type on or before the stock's sale date.

Companies are needed to show the papers that track their trading work. The SEC's website provides restricted access to these papers, but also for higher access, check out among some company that reports expert trading information, such as www.marketwatch.com and www.bloomberg.com.

## Sarbanes-Oxley Act

In the stock market mania of 1997-- 2000, this misuse had not been simply limited to insider purchasing and selling of stock; it also covered the relevant abuse of bookkeeping scams. Because insiders are primarily the top administration, they tricked investors about the financial conditions of the business and subsequently were able to raise the perceived

The stock might, after that, be sold at a rate that was higher than market value. SOX established a public audit oversight board and tightened the policies on company economic reporting.

The insider must wait at least six months before getting it once more. The rule is likewise real if an expert sells the stock. An expert can't sell it at a higher cost within six months.

Checking Out Insider Transactions
Analyzing insider acquiring against expert marketing can be as different as day and night. Expert buying is comfortable, while insider marketing can be complicated.

## Knowing from insider buying

Expert purchasing is usually a distinct signal about how an insider feels about his company. Besides, the key reason that all investors buy a stock is that they expect it to do well. That's generally not a considerable occasion if one expert is buying inventory. But if more experts are getting, those acquisitions should capture your attention.

Expert acquiring is usually a positive omen and advantageous for the stock's rate. When insiders buy stock, less stock is offered to the public. If the investing public meets this lowered stock with enhanced demand, then the

stock price surges. Keep these factor in mind when analyzing expert buying:

Knowing who is buying the stock.

The CEO is buying 5,000 shares. Is that reason enough for you to jump in? Maybe. After all, the CEO knows how well the performance of the company. What if before this purchase, she had no stock in the company at all? Maybe the stock is part of her employment package.

The truth that a new business executive is making her first stock acquisition isn't as strong a signal urging you to buy as the fact that a veteran CEO is doubling her holdings. If significant numbers of insiders are buying, that sends out a more reliable signal than if a single expert is buying.

See how much is being bought.

In the instance in the previous section, the CEO bought 5,000 shares, which is a whole lot of stock, no matter how you count it. But is it enough for you to base a financial investment decision on? Maybe, but a closer look may reveal more. Getting 5,000 additional shares would not be h a good signal of a pending stock increase if she currently owned 1 million shares at the time of the purchase. In this instance, 5,000 shares are a small step-by-step step and don't offer much to get excited able.

What if this insider has possessed just 5,000 shares for the past three years and is now getting 1 million shares? Generally, a significant acquisition tells you that a particular insider has a solid sense of the firm's leads and that she's making a substantial increase in her share of stock possession.

100,000 shares each. Once more, if someone is purchasing, that might or may not be a secure sign of a future increase. If many people are getting, consider it an incredible indicator.

"The more, the merrier!" is an excellent regulation for judging expert buying. All these people have their unique viewpoints on the business and its leads for the near future. Mass buying means mass positivity for the future of the company. If the treasurer, the head of state, the vice-president of sales, and many other principals are placing their extensive range on the line and investing it in a business that they know carefully, that's an excellent sign for your stock investment also.

Notice the timing of the purchase. The timing of expert stock purchases is vital too. If I inform you that five insiders got stock at various points in 2014, you might say, "Hmm." But if I tell you that all the five people got chunks of stock at the same time and right before earnings period, that must make you say, "HMMMMM!".

Picking up tips from Insider marketing.

Insider stock purchasing is hardly an unfavorable event.

Experts may sell their stock for a pair factors: They might assume that the company will not be doing well in the close to future-- an unfavorable sign for you-- or they might simply need the money for a range of individual factors that have nothing to do with the firm's possibility. Some typical reasons experts may sell stock include the following:

To diversify their holdings. If an insider's portfolio is slowly heavy with one firm's stock, a monetary consultant may recommend that he balance his portfolio by marketing a few of that business's stock and purchasing different other protections.

To finance personal emergencies. Often an insider needs money for medical, legal, or family reasons.

To buy a home or make one more major acquisition. An expert may need the cash to make a down settlement or maybe to buy something outright without having to get a car loan.

How do you get information about insider stock selling?

Although experts should report their essential stock sales and acquisitions to the SEC, the information isn't always disclosing.

Always answer these questions before assessing insider marketing:

How numerous insiders are marketing?

If just one expert is marketing, that one deal does not give you enough info to act on.

Is the usual pattern showing on the sales? If one expert offered some stock last month, that sale alone isn't that considered an occasion. However, if ten insiders have made several sales in the past few months, those sales are the reason for the issue. See whether any type of new developments at the business is possibly harmful. Consider placing a stop-loss order on your stock immediately if substantial expert selling has recently happened, and you don't know why.

How much stock is being sold?

That's not a big deal if a CEO markets 5,000 shares of stock but still saves 100,000 shares. If the CEO sells all or a lot of his holdings, that's a possible adverse. Examine to see whether various other business execs have additionally sold the stock.

Do outdoor events or analyst records appear accidental with the sale of the stock? Often, an influential analyst might release a report cautioning about a firm's potential customers. If the company's administration waves aside the record buy the majority of them are bailing out anyhow (marketing their stock), you may wish to do the same. Regularly, when experts understand that dam maturing information looms, they sell the stock before it takes a dip.

In the same way, if the company's management issues positive public declarations or reports that are contradictory to their habits (they're selling their stock holdings), the SEC might investigate to see whether the company is doing anything that may need a charge. The SEC regularly tracks expert sales.

## Considering Corporate Stock Buybacks.

When you review the monetary web pages or watch the financial programs on television, you sometimes listen to how a company is getting its very stock.

When companies buy back their stock, they're generally showing that they believe their stock is underestimated, which can increase. If a business reveals strong fundamentals (for instance, excellent economic condition and enhancing earnings and sales) and it's purchasing more of its stock, it's worth exploring it may make a fantastic enhancement to your portfolio.

If you see that a business is buying back its stock while many of the experts are selling their shares, that's not the right signal. It might not necessarily be a wrong signal, yet it's not a favorable indication. Play it risk-free and spend elsewhere.

The following areas present some typical factors a company might redeem its shares from investors in addition to some ideas on the negative results of stock buybacks.

- Enhancing revenues per share

By only redeeming its shares from investors, a business can enhance its revenues per share without having extra money. Sound like an illusionist's technique? Well, it is, type of. A company stock buyback is a monetary deception that investors should know.

Right here's how it works:

NEI has 10 million shares, and it's expected to web profits of $10 million for the 4th quarter. NEI's revenues per share (EPS) would be $1 per share. Thus far, so excellent. However, what happens.

If NEI buys two million of its shares? Total shares impressive shrink to 8 million. The new EPS is $1.25-- the stock buyback synthetically improves the earnings per share by 25 percent!

The crucial sign about stock buybacks is that real company profits do not change-- no essential changes happen in business monitoring or procedures-- so the increase in EPS can be deceptive.

The market can be compulsive about incomes, and because profits are the lifeblood of any company, an earnings increase, even if it's cosmetic, can also increase the stock price.

Also, a stock buyback influences stock and need. With less available stock on the market, demand always sends the stock rate upwards.

Whenever a firm makes a significant purchase, such as acquiring back its stock, think about just how the firm is paying for it and whether it looks like an excellent use of the company's purchasing power. In basic, companies buy their stock for the same factors any investor purchases stock-- they think that the stock is an excellent financial investment and will appreciate in time.

**Beating back a takeover quote.**

Because acquiring and offering stock are done in a public market or exchange, companies can buy each other's stock. In some cases, the target company likes not to be obtained, in which instance it might buy its shares of stock to protect it against unwanted actions by interested companies.

In most cases, the firm trying the requisition already possesses some of the target business's stock. In this case, the targeted firm may want to repurchase those shares from the aggressor at a premium to prevent the requisition proposal. This kind of deal is frequently described as greenmail.

Takeover usually worries rapid interest in the investing public, driving the stock cost upward and benefiting present stockholders.

**Checking out the drawback of buybacks.**

If a business pays for the stock with investments from operations, it may comprise of unfavorable effect on the company's ability to fund reasonable and current processes. In general, any mismanagement of money, such as using financial obligation to repurchase stock, influences a company's capability to grow its sales and profits-- two measures that need to keep higher mobility to maintain stock prices climbing.

Why does business split their stock?

Generally, management thinks that the stock's price is high, thus potentially discouraging investors from buying it. The stock split is a way to stir the rate of interest in the stock, and this boost interest regularly leads to an increase in the stock's price.

Getting approved for a stock split is similar to certified to receive a return; you have to be noted as an investor as the date of record.

A stock split is technically a neutral occasion because the supreme market value of the company's stock does not change as a result of the separation.

The following sections give both fundamental kinds of splits: average and reverse stock splits.

1.  Average stock divides.

When the number of stock shares increases- we usually hear about this, average stock splits--. (For example, a 2-for-1 stock split increases the number of shares.) If you possess 100 shares of Dublin, Inc., stock (at $60 per share), and the investment shows a stock split, what happens? You receive in the mail a stock certification for if you have the stock in certificate kind.

One hundred shares of Dublin, Inc. no, before you think of how your money will double, examine the stock's new price. Each share is changed to a $30 worth.

Not all stock is in certificate kind. Stocks held in a brokerage firm account are taped in book-entry variety. Most stock, in reality, is in book entrance type.

A business only issues stock certificates when necessary or when the investor asks for it. Always consult your broker for the new share total amount to make sure that you're qualified with the original number of shares after the stock split.

A stock split is mainly a neutral occasion, so why does a company bother to do it? One of the most common reasons is that monitoring thinks that the stock is also pricey, so it intends to decrease the stock price to make the stock extra affordable and, for that reason, more attractive to new financiers. Research has shown that stock splits often precede a rise in the stock rate. Although stock divides are thought about a non-event in and of themselves, lots of stock experts see them as favorable signals as a result of the interest they produce among the investing public.

## 2. Reverse stock splits

A reverse stock split generally happens when a company management wants to increase the rate of its stock. If a stock's cost looks too low, that might discourage passion by specific or institutional investors (such as stock funds). The management intends to drum up more interest in the stock for the advantage of investors (a few of whom are probably insiders).

The firm might also do a reverse split to reduce expenses. When you have to send a yearly record and other correspondence regularly to all the stock- owners, the mailings can get a little expensive, particularly when you have many investors that have a few shares each. Reverse split helps to consolidate the shares to reduced overall management expenses.

A reverse split can best be clarified with an example. TCI introduces a 10-for-1 reverse stock split. If an existing investor had 100 shares at $2 (the old shares), the stockholder currently possesses ten stocks at $20.

Technically, a reverse split is known as a neutral event. Simply as financiers might assume favorable expectations from an ordinary stock split, they may have negative assumptions from a reverse split, because a reverse split tends to happen for negative reasons.

If, on the occasion of a stock split, you have a weird number of shares, the company does not create a "fractional share."Instead, you have to look for the money matching.

Keep good records about your stock splits in case you need to calculate capital gains tax.

# CHAPTER TWELVE

## How to Identify a Stock that is About to Explode Higher

### Essential tools to identify if a stock is about to explode

" Typically, when a stock gets overbought, it is ripe for a pullback because overbought stocks, ones with lots of buyers reaching to absorb the stock, often tend to break back after they have gotten as far away from their longer-term trend line," the CNBC host said.

Financiers can determine whether a stock is overbought or oversold by charting the ratio of higher closes, likewise called the family member power index, or RSI. This is a momentum oscillator that processes the instructions of a given stock and the speed of its step.

To find times in a specific stock's trajectory where its toughness sticks out-- a possible sign of a pending revocation or change in momentum-- Cramer matches the stock's RSI to something else, such as the loved one strength of its sector or a broader index, and afterward determines the past cost action.

But the inverse can also be real, as a stock can fall so quickly that investors should expect it to break back because it is practically oversold, claims the "Mad Money" host. These trends are positive signs that a change in instructions is about to happen and tend to be stellar activity points.

So, for investors that are debating whether they should buy a stock and have done all the research to discover that the said stock is overbought, Cramer recommends waiting on the inescapable pullback that often takes place.

Some stocks, but can break through all the generally determined ceilings and stay overbought for weeks at a time.

" They oppose the notion of the unavoidable gravitational pull of the old stability line and can't be restricted by any of the many ceilings that overbought problems generally bump right into," Cramer said. "When you find these unusual actions, you may have the ability to band yourself into an actual moonshot."

Quantity is one more crucial tool that chartists use to find pivots. It is usually said that number can be a lie detector for investors to inform if a move is real or otherwise. When a little relocation happens in light quantity, service technicians neglect it.

If huge money managers are starting to build or distribute the stock in a hostile means, chartists make use of volume to establish.

Professionals likewise measure something called an accumulation circulation line. This involves charting whether a stock shuts greater on better quantity on any given day, against lower, or on the reduced amount.

Most brokerage firm companies stock this type of charting on their websites. While Cramer considers the method to be somewhat mysterious, he trusts funds because it goes against the grain of conventional thinking and provides a new way to take a look at stock motions.

Cramer saw this happen with shares of Monsanto in July 2012. He didn't worry about the stock of the company at the time; the buildup circulation line showed that the stock had fall days with light volume and rise days with dark volume.

To Cramer, that was a particular sign that more money was streaming into the stock rather than out of it.

It ends up that Monsanto's stock had started correlating with the price of corn, which was going higher due to the new demand for ethanol brought about by government cost assistance. Cramer was too worried about near-term profits and bothered with a deficiency to acknowledge what was happening.

" Powerful relocations can, and commonly do avoid those that are just concentrated on the underlying business and not the activity of the stocks themselves," Cramer said.

# CHAPTER 13

Forecasting how the stock exchange is going to be in a year, 2021 is going to prove to be one of the most different years on record, because of how outrageous 2020 has been.

The directions to buy and sell stocks in a specific business will be given through a brokerage firm. This information will be handed down to those trading to connect the agreed rate and commodity to the buyer and seller. All the transactions done might be within a matter of seconds and can involve a substantial amount of cash.

During the different timeframe, varieties of stocks are traded, which can either be preferred stock and typical stock.

Right now, most of the economy is facing one challenge or the other; a lot of countries are left to deal with the recession in a few years to come. Since it was a disastrous occurrence, and lots of services have been lost.

Of course, this is going to have a current effect on the stock exchange too. While some stocks have remained reasonably stable, with some even continuing to grow throughout this duration, it's clear that companies who are more most likely to be impacted have been noted down.

When predicting the stock exchange in 2021, there are some factors one needs to consider:

One possibility is that the stock exchange will see something which is described as V-shaped recovery, which indicates that although it has declined in the last few months, it will bounce back by the 4th quarter of the year.

Some predicted that the coronavirus does not appear to be slowing, because the financial repercussions of the infection could open other market opportunities.

This might work towards filling deep space that's been created by the declining shares of various businesses. Besides, many investors who saw substantial losses due to their financial investments in more delicate companies will now pump money into riskier properties to attempt and regain a few of their momentum.

Most countries are following the same pattern with central banks stepping in to guarantee that the force to the stock exchange is not as dangerous as it could be and therefore reducing the fears of investors and making them less likely to back out.

No one knows how this will play out as we get closer and closer to 2021. What we do understand for sure is that the world is a different place to what it was the last time we saw a market crash of this magnitude.

The virus may still be with us by this time next year, that the affected organization will always have shares that have completely plunged, however, the market itself will have stabilized since of the aid of institutions such as the federal reserve as well as the modified approach of financiers.

New York stock exchange is one of the most significant stock trading homes in the world, and the analysis record about USD153 billion traded daily.

The "buying and selling" is done at a rapid and energetic speed, and the awareness of an individual plays a huge role in getting the deals done according to the requirements of clients. These "clients" or customers typically appoint brokers to do the trading on their behalf in some cases with particular standards and some leaving the decisions to the discretion of the brokers employed.

If you are planning to invest in 2021, you should have in mind that there are specific stocks which will be more reputable. Choose for yourself whether it's more worth going for dividend-yielding stocks or bonds. Think about software application business and financial markets over retail and commodities.

Do your research study, listen to the experts, and keep as approximate date as possible on which stocks are succeeding and which ones are going to stop working, and one needs to maintain some strong investments.

## Steps InTaking Advantage Of Online Opportunities

However, identifying the changes that will ultimately yield the wanted earnings or income, might take skill and understanding that must be carefully considered as such chances posture some level of dangers. Business savvy individuals are likewise always on the lookout for service changes that will bring them more money. Being informed and keeping abreast of all the most recent developments assists in guaranteeing a person to be current.

- **Inspect Out The Stock Market**

For the brave individual aiming the stock market for chances to generate income is a practical choice; because sometimes it is a dangerous option to choose. One needs to constantly be well geared up with the relevant knowledge to ensure the best stocks and opportunities are spotted.

- **Investing**

Being an entity that supplies services from stockbroking to trading in other securities, you should understand that the stock market can be extremely unpredictable in its negotiations.

Keep the focus on little and fast profits rather than attempting to get rich overnight. A lot of people lack the knowledge of when to buy and when to sell. Buying is generally based on the beliefs of the time, and some experience, selling is primarily based upon individual perception.

When the stock price is appreciating, we get tempted to see it climb higher before entering it. This is a very harmful line of thought as the stock cost can fall just as quickly as it went up, triggering extraordinary unfavorable repercussions. A limit ought to be set early on in the buying phase so, when this preset limit is fulfilled, the stock can be entered. The limit set will help in decreasing any possible losses—Avoidgoing after an upward trend without the pertinent lacking understanding of the business.

- **Identify Your Objectives.**

Pursuing opportunities with the intent of earning or getting a respectable amount of earnings ought to be done with some percentage of constant caution.

Your strategy should be able to identify the extent of opportunities that would produce the wanted revenue within the desired amount of time.

This is to guarantee the interest levels are kept consistent and hence developing the needed "buzz" to keep the private concentrated on the goal till the wanted results are accomplished. Understanding the expectation will also assist the person in being able to select the opportunities that would be well suited towards achieving the set goals.

These objectives may vary from individual to individual as the majority of people have their concepts on what they deem to be successful.

Being more open-minded and attentive permits a person to be more conscious of any opportunities that might develop as the unpleasantness of always missing out on the chance boat ends up being a norm.

# CHAPTER 14

## Understanding the software and Online BrokerForStockmarket

An online search on the web will reveal to you that there are many online brokers and representatives out there that desire you to patronize them. Considering that the electronic trading market initially was created in 1994, e-brokers have established organizations to assist you. These e-brokers aim to take over the market at less expensive rates. They compete both with standard offline brokers and also with other online brokers.

There are lots of to select from, and they all appear to provide what you need. Always do your research by asking people their thoughts about the broker you are thinking about, take your time in selecting a broker. If you know, there will be a particular time that you will probably require your broker to make sure that their website is available both day and night. You must also discover how long it usually takes there site to load during peak times. Absolutely nothing is more annoying than needing to make an essential trade and being unable to fill the website to do so online!

Below are some essential things you need to decide on before getting involved with an online trading Broker:

**Price to trade and purchase**

- Do you know what amount to acquire and trade stocks online?
- Do you know when the best time to purchase and when to sell?

When deciding, these are all things a good investor needs to be familiar with financial investment choices. Learn what to look for, what to avoid, fees to expect, and more.

**Portfolios**

How to keep and develop a portfolio to work correctly for you. You are constructing an online portfolio, updating it, checking your stocks online, and more.

## Costs and fees

What costs you can expect and which ones can be reduced or prevented entirely. What do you need to pay to start trading or to access a particular kind of

trade? Another element of choosing an online broker is what type of client service they have to offer.

## Types Of Brokers

Do you understand that there are several kinds of online brokers? A basic search engine will bring up the enormous result of different companies and alternatives that are out there. So how can you fully understand which one to choose? But note that all online brokers are not the same.

Different brokers offer different features before a person can begin to understand the kinds of brokers and which one is best to fulfill your needs, firstly, you will need to know the different types of brokers.

Different kinds of brokers offer different levels of support and services. A broker that will deal with their customer directly is called a routine broker. Broker resellers are middle-men that goes between you, as a customer and a larger broker company.

There are four basic categories of online brokers that you can find. We are going to list and explain them below so that you understand what you are searching for. Below are the types of brokers:

1. Discount rate brokers/online brokers

2. Assisted discount rate broker

3. Complete broker

4. Money manager/financial advisor

Now let us dive into these four types of brokers to know what are their specific tasks, and how do you understand which one do you need for your online trading usage?

## 1. Discount/Online Brokers

The online discount broker is essentially just an order taker. You put in the trade that you wish to make, and they position it for you, usually online, although some take orders over the phone as well. You will not receive assistance or guidance from your discount broker.

Remember that while discount brokers will save you cash, it will be at the expenditure of little or no assistance whatsoever. You might discover some discount rates or online brokers that offer support with researchers. However, it is generally through a third party and will cost you more cash through that third party.

## 2. Assisted Discount Broker

An assisted discount broker will provide you a bit more than a non-assisted online broker. Precisely just how much help they offer differs, and you will need to talk to them first to see how much support a particular service provides you. They use diverse methods that do not leave you entirely on your own but don't offer a complete either. Their websites will usually have more details of them, how you can get in contact, and some may likewise have newsletters and other techniques of offering you investing help. They will generally supply you with the necessary information and not specific stock ideas.

### 3. Complete Broker

This broker will provide several specific services as a standard offline broker. They will give you guidance and suggestions on particular stocks. They will be available to offer you tips, advice, hints, pointers, and assistance through the trading procedure. They will begin with an evaluation of your financial scenario to help identify your requirements and what investment opportunities are best for you.

A complete broker will help put together a portfolio that fulfills your needs and desires and your financial capabilities at this time.

## 4. Money Manager/Financial Advisor

A money manager or financial consultant deals with specific requirements. They may often likewise be called by other names. Generally, they manage more significant portfolios such as those financiers coping with large amounts of money to be invested. Money managers are trained to take obligation for investing and managing substantial portfolios. An excellent cash manager will be expensive, but for better reasons, it worth it.

Always put into consideration the different kinds of brokers and choose only the one that fulfills your requirements the best. Always ensure your broker is covered by the Securities Investor Protection Corporation, which will protect your possessions in a brokerage that represents up to $500,000 in case the firm stops working. This insurance coverage is significant, specifically with a lot of brokers online these days. Ensurethat whoever you decide, you feel comfy with them and that you can trust them to deal with something as sensitive and your money and financial investments.

## Selecting An Online Broker

Selecting an online broker is an important decision only like in traditional trading; you would consider your broker important. There are lots of" discount rate" online brokers that merely do not have your best interests in mind. You need to find out how to search the right brokers that need to be prevented and how to choose the one that will work best for you appropriately. Some factors to consider when deciding on a broker selection involves:

- Client service

You understand that client service is an essential element of your broker when making trades online or offline. Nothing is more annoying than not having access to speak with a live person when you have a problem or challenge, especially with something that deals with your cash. Even if you choose an abasic discount broker that you will not usually consult with, you still need to know where and what their customer care contacts are so that when you need them, you can call them instantly.

If consumer service is necessary to you, you will want to avoid those brokers that don't have a great, quality customer care system in place. You will thoroughly search if you care about consumer service of high quality.

- Online Broker Fees.

Broker fees are probably among the first things you inquire about when you wish to select a broker. However, to make a great choice about whether a specific broker service is providing you a reasonable offer, you need to understand what the fees are for in the very first place. You must comprehend what they are all for; you need a breakdown of the online broker fees. You must know what the standard charges are, along with what you are being charged for and why you need to pay the charges. This is very important so that you are not scammed or overcharged. Also, be careful of a discount broker that does not offer you any guide about its investment.

A person who has acquired enough trading experience on their own may be able to manage using a service like this; if you are not prepared to do the research study and leg work involved with investing, then it would be smarter to use a full-service broker.

A complete broker will supply you with essential details that are required to make a wise investment decision. They handle most of the tasks involved and will provide you their opinion on what they believe would and would not be an excellent financial investment.

When considering broker fees from a firm, Below are some more suggestions you must know, whether online or offline.

- Minimal cost.

Most brokers have a minimal charge that they will charge for opening an online brokerage account. These charges typically range between $5-40 per trade, depending on how the trade is made. There might also be a minimum range to the number of shares you can buy to secure that estimated cost. Make sure you always read the small print to see if there are other specifications included. Inspect the advertisement or contract to see if it states which services the marketed rate will entitle you to. In most cases, there will be higher costs for limitation orders, options, and those trades over the phone with your broker. The marketed commission rate may not use to the kind of trade you desire to execute.

## Deposits.

Most businesses require high minimum balances for opening your account; some companies will desire as much as $10,000 to begin. The cheap services will get you a low-cost item, you will likely not have any help, and customer service might not even be trusted or customer friendly. If you know what you are targeting, you may be comfortable with a broker like this; however, if you require more assistance with your trades, you will just be irritated with inexpensive online broker services.

## Product Selection And Other Bonus.

Prices shouldn't be the only point you desire to consider when you are looking to pick an online broker. Product choice is also very essential, because not every broker provides every service and every kind of trade. You have to be 100% sure that the broker you are aiming to use deals with the types of trades that you wish to place.

In addition to the product itself, there are other "bonus" that you will desire to consider and look to see if a specific brokerage service provides it. While many people select a broker based upon the reality that they desire to purchase stocks, you also require to bear in mind that other investment options might not be available through every broker. You need to inspect what you want, such as:

- CDs.

- Municipal bonds.

- Futures.

- Options.

- Gold/silver certificates.

- Commodities, and more.

You will wish to select a broker that offers you these alternatives in addition to many trading stocks. You may get in on a great offer with a broker online just to find that later when you go to purchase another type of financial investment, they don't use it. It's more preferable for you to choose a broker at the beginning that will use different options you need and desire. Ensure you check out this completely, so you do not end up not having the ability to make the trades that you want.

Another thing to search for is a return on cash. This will mean that you are most likely always to have some quantity of money in your brokerage account. Just how much will depend on the particular broker; however, a standard amount has to do with 3-5% interest on the money.

**Automated Stock Software**
Stock market trading is uninterruptedly evolving and is more than a handful of reasons that technology firms and developers have come up with software or unique computer programs that are aimed at ultimately gearing up the modern stock market trader and financier.

Taking a peek at the modern-day and newest stock trading software application readily available online is commendable.

When buying a stock trading software, below are some standard features you need to look for online.

- **The Ticker.**

You would see tickers when you see organization news channels. A ticker includes business names and the equivalent stock rate that goes with the stock at present. Tickers are practical to financiers and brokers because they suggest whether a stock is decreasing or is rising.

- **The Stock predictor.**

Since there are tickers, stock rates are taped in the archives. Hence, analysis of daily and every hour movements of stock rates would help presume and anticipate a specific stock future and possible stock rate movements.

- **The Currency converter.**

Because foreign investments or cross-border investments can now be possible, there are different kinds of stock trading software applications that consist of currency converters to track their financial investments against their local currencies correctly.

Obviously, similar to anything you acquire and download online, you must exercise optimum prudence and note that not all items that are being used are, in fact, dependable. Do your research by checking out consumer evaluations and ask around about the software.

- **Business Online Software.**

Software application designers have come up with special software or computer system programs that are created to equip modern-day stock exchange traders and investors. The fast increase in population development and the number of industrial stock financiers are motivating. This offers a wide range of opportunities for businesses that focus on the advancement of software for each unique need.

- **Chart Tool.**

A graphical tool that uses stock cost information; this information is then converted into maps so that the analyst, the viewer, or the investor can quickly keep an eye on and manage the movements of specific stocks. That makes life a lot simpler for these operations.

- **Currency.**

Since cross-border financial investment or foreign financial investment is now possible, there are numerous stock trading software applications on the marketplace, that include currency converters.

In today's market, investors are asking if they need even to buy stocks as well as if they can generate income. The solution to both is "yes." Stock market trading is a terrific chance currently, with costs lower as well as volatility higher than in years.

There are many automated trading platforms of robotic trading programs, on the internet, the best way to define the supply trading systems that can help you to make a supply financial investment and to expand your cash. Review the criteria below and recognize your personal preferences by speaking with other stock traders

Lots of kinds of firms provide stock trading suggestions as well as stock trading methods. They run a program aiming to teach you how to trade, to a listing of suggested supplies to deal with specific triggers, to broker agent firm proprietary software program, all the way to wholly automated robotic software. The cost can be from hundreds of dollars to less than $50 a month for some automobile trading software. This chapter will direct you via the functions and advantages of the programs that are available for online supply trading.

A lot of the programs are geared in the direction of "day investors," that practically open lengthy settings (buy) or short positions (sell short) as well as shut these settings the same day. Not everyone that uses these programs closes out their settings by the end of the trading day-- occasionally they hold their placements for days, weeks, or months.

The vital functions of a supply trading program contain information feed for supply quotes and indicators, stock charts or charting ability of primary indications, current balance, and settings and an order entry system. The order access system should enable quit (loss) orders, quit limit orders, and tracking stops. A tracking stop limit is similar to the quit (loss), other than its loss will undoubtedly be measured from the supply's highest point attained. The favored method would certainly be to keep the trigger costs in stealth setting, not viewable by the market makers, instead of as real orders. A lot of automated trading software ought to include a watch checklist of the supplies to possibly trade based upon the specifications the supply investor has gotten in.

## Inspect the Features and also Ask Questions

Number of Technical Indicators

Numerous indicators supply investors can make use of to determine which stocks to deal as well as when. The most durable programs will certainly use innumerable indications for technical evaluation, such as Bollinger Bands, as well as some, will certainly even consist of indications for Candlestick Chart developments. Robot programs use these indicators to establish conditions under which online investing will happen.

Intricacy.

Some online stock trading systems do require real programming knowledge. Check out the demo online to see that it fits your level of comfort before making any commitment. Speak to others that are currently using automated trading sites and check them up on the internet for more comments.

### Different Long and Short Strategies Per Account

If you wish to run, claim two lengthy trading methods, then you may require two accounts. Additionally, validate if you have enough memory on your computer system for two or even more accounts. Experienced energetic investors might run two or more real-time long and short methods while having extra make up techniques that they are evaluating in a simulator setting.

### Advised Additional Features

The best-automated supply trading software will certainly consist of additional functions that energetic investors will locate indispensable once they have begun computerized trading.

Additional strategy and also order access functions consist of the ability to add to a position as a stock rises, or as the stock declines, in addition to a minimal acquisition interval that the stock price should go down before it begins buying added shares. A maximum bid/ask range will also be handy, as the size of the spread can straight influence a swing investor's ability to make profitable professions. The meaning or formula for signs may vary from one electronic trading system to another, so make sure you understand them first.

Advise you have a program that presents existing Profit and also Loss (P&L) on your dashboard

Some automated stock trading programs aesthetically present the portion of icons up and down in each industry from the defined period to the present time so you can see exactly how the marketplace is transforming. Does the system include the capability to obstruct certain symbols from trading? If you're running a lengthy trading approach, you won't intend to be buying ETFs in the market.

Day traders will want automatic trading software that tracks and also presents the number of day trades continuing to be. Day trading is controlled by the SEC, so it's crucial to comprehend if you will be day trading initially.

## How to Create A Stock Trading Strategy

There should be a step by step to follow through to show newbie traders exactly how to create a trading technique. Are there off-the-shelf techniques that are offered for your usage? Exist any costs included, or are they supplied utterly free? Can you modify the off the shelf methods? Keep in mind that firms should not be ensuring you a guaranteed return. The very best companies will have long and also brief supply trading strategies readily available at the house and will surely enable the stock investor to create their own. Some companies will also allow you to duplicate strategy from a "buddies" checklist. One dimension does not fit all. If the company doesn't inform you of the details of the procedure or why they selected or advise a particular stock, after that, it's not suggested to utilize it. You may be paying too much for "proprietary" services and also may have the ability to obtain free securities market pointers and suggestions online that will do comparably.

## Technical Support and Clients Service

Outstanding automated stock trading software program firms have a very huge "up-time" and also are exceptionally rarely out of service. Look at the company's document, just how commonly have they had failures? The software application needs to be simple to set up and also should work with a selection of running systems (Windows XP, Windows Vista, and so on). If you have inquiries, are there experienced and also helpful personnel to provide a solution? Just how promptly do they respond, if by email?

## Compensations

Trading payments can eat into your earnings if you are not careful regarding picking a strategy that fits your demands. Compensations can differ greatly from broker to broker, relying on the number of shares traded, whether the shares are in rounded lots of 100, the cost of the shares traded as well as the variety of trades you put every month.

Stock traders might also want to have more than one account if they have a trading method that typically trades 100 shares whole lots, and even one more that trades a thousand share great deals. It pays to read them thoroughly.

## Variety Of Broker Options

If you have an exclusive broker agent software, then you'll only have the ability to trade with that firm. The best online trading consists of the most affordable compensations for the regular professions for every technique that you utilize. There are various other programs whose software program has been incorporated into the order putting functionality at a selection of broker agent companies.

Prices will vary by company, well-known companies with the most affordable commissions will not pay you or provide a cash market fund for your unvested cash. This is just how they maintain their prices down. If you anticipate having additional cash that you will not make use of for trading, you might intend to keep it in another account where it can gain much more. You should also inspect if there is a minimum to open an account or a minimum number of trades called for.

## Examine the Costs and also Software Support

Subscription fee - Is there likewise a month-to-month fee? If so, what does it cover? In assessing online trading solutions, more expensive software is not necessarily far better. Some energetic investing services are less costly because they have more clients.

Information Feed Fee - Does the program consist of real-time data feeds for stock quotes as well as an indicator? Exists an extra charge for this, or is it consisted of in the fundamental monthly fee? This is the most significant component price in developing computerized stock trading programs.

Long-term Contract - Is the fee you're paying in advance for a year's contract? If so, is it immediately restored every year?

Training Fee - For programs that market themselves as monetary instructors, there will be a charge, in some cases hundreds or countless bucks, as this is exactly how they make their cash. The most effective automated supply trading software application gives free training.

Educating Formats - Is the training in the form of a real-time seminar? Webinar? Exist extra materials such as DVD's that you must buy to figure out all the information marketed? Or is online training readily available in the business's office?

Minimum to Invest - Brokerage companies have their minimums; however, there are additionally account minimum balances required by the Securities and Exchange Commission (SEC) wherefore it calls "pattern day traders." A day profession occurs when a trader opens as well as closes the same setting in a margin account on the very same day.

The average accurate range indicator
This is an essential indicator that can be used for setting stops and is also another way of measuring volatility and is consisted of most software systems.

The daily ATR indication is straightforward to calculate as it checks through the volatility of the market over a period and is the highest of:

- The difference between the present high and the present low
- The distinction between the present high and the previous close
- The distinction between the current low and the previous close

The average is then taken control of a set variety of days (ten is often used), and the stop is then determined as a multiple of the ATR. The aim traders prefer the ATR is that it captures more intra-day details, while the standard deviation only measures the volatility of closing rates (although it can be fine-tuned to consist of highs, lows, etc.).

# CHAPTER 15

# Random Behaviour in the Stockmarket

Throughout the years, there has been much research work that intended to learn if market action was random or whether there was evidence that it could be anticipated regularly. Different relevant documents have revealed distinct repeating patterns both in cost and time cycles, which efficiently validate that market action is not random.

Charts frequently exhibit comparable pattern behavior in indices, forex, treasury bonds, and products, along with share prices. Nonetheless, there are times when the action does appear haphazard, and the description for this is what is called the 'random walk theory.'

Random strolls and efficient markets

There have been three main works that attempted to 'describe' random action. A researcher called Burton Malkiel stated that "A Random Walk Down Wall Street," which has turned into one of the most well-known financial investment works. The book said on his stock market theory in which he specified that the previous motion or instructions of the cost of a stock or general market might not be used to forecast its future movement.

He stated that the active market consisted of many well notified and smart financiers, securities would be appropriately priced. They would show all readily available information, and if the market was efficient, no news or analysis might be expected to result in the outperformance of proper criteria. In the market, there were great deals of contending players, with each trying to predict the future market price of private securities.

This would lead to a scenario where existing rates of individual securities currently showed the results of details based both on events that have currently taken place and those that were anticipated to occur in the future.

**Efficient Market Hypothesis was seen to have three forms:**

The "**Weak**" type asserted that all past market value and information were completely reflected in securities costs. Technical analysis was of no use.

The "**Semi strong**" type declared that all publicly available info was reflected in securities prices. In other words, the essential analysis was of no use.

The "**Strong**" type asserted that all info was fully reflected in securities prices. In other words, even insider information was of no use.

Those three kinds efficiently dismiss all analyses as futile, whether it be technical or fundamental. Undoubtedly when a trader takes a position, this is based upon a view of mispricing in their favor, and in this respect, there have been lots of papers proving that the marketplace is certainly not random A glimpse at chart books from the 1970s for circumstances frequently shows incredibly similar price action to that seen on current charts. Again similar patterns are often visible to forex and product traders.

## The other view - the marketplace is not random.

The problem in attempting to prove that the marketplace is not random is that a technique that might work for a statistically valid period of analysis might suddenly get bad once it is extensively understood because the edge the trader might have had in pricing will be negated to numerous individuals, which will influence the opening and closing price.

### RiskandVolatility in Stockmarket Trading
Which is often puzzled with risk if there is one area that is routinely overlooked by CFD traders, it is that of volatility. In terms of grading different types of possession classes, the two are connected, and both the risk and volatility of government stock.

Volatility nevertheless determines just how much rates rise or fall over a set time for each investment sector, or share, and this is exceptionally beneficial when building portfolios, evaluating margin requirements and position sizing.

### What is beta?

Beta is another procedure of volatility, and while completely different from underlying variance, it, however, provides another angle in portfolio or trade building.

Standard deviation identifies the volatility of a fund, sector, market, or stock according to the variation of its returns over some time, whereas beta figures out the volatility in contrast to an index or other benchmark.

This suggests that the list should typically match the underlying movement in that standard over time if a financier has a portfolio of shares with a beta of 1. It doesn't imply that it will naturally be better or even worse on a specific stock basis.

Every single stock has a beta, which is essential for CFD traders, and a beta of more than 1 suggests higher volatility than the benchmark, with a beta of less than one recommending a low volatility.

A beta two stock would be expected to move two times more than the standard, or double the hidden index relocation. If a trader has the option of going shorts and longs, the average beta on each side needs to be examined in terms of the total risk of significant market moves in one direction.

Usually, not always, the highest beta stocks are those with the most significant volatility as measured by the standard discrepancy, but also how much they are affected by the business cycle and rate of interest. Fund supervisors, housebuilders, and insurers, for example, have much greater betas than grocery stores, pharmaceuticals, and energy stocks.

When analyzing the portfolio, the coefficient of beta(level of sensitivity of the asset returns to market returns and relative volatility), is a critical criterion in the capital possession pricing design and is a way of separating an investor's profits related to market action instead of the determination to take a threat. In essence, this suggests how much-added value there has been rather than simply the luck from being in increasing markets.

It is best to select high beta stocks if one is highly bullish about the underlying market. Similarly, if a huge fall is expected imminently, a CFD trader may prefer to take low beta long positions and high beta shorts if a well-balanced trading list was needed.

# CHAPTER 16

## Techniques To Beat Stock Barriers And Obstacles

It has been stated that you must "deal with the important things you fear, and you eliminate that worry."Fear is an ingredient of life; different individuals have different types of worry. Some have shallow fears; others have intense fears. Concerns are normal, especially if a good amount of cash is at stake, ought to be overwhelmed by barriers. With this, you need to believe in ways to beat the obstacles and required methods for a successful day trading.

- **Educate yourself.**

There is no much better way to prepare you into beating the barriers than informing yourself. When you are now familiar with the dos and don't of day trading, then you can be confident that you will win, if not half the battle or all of it. You need to comprehend the day trading market.

- **Plan ahead.**

Considering that many people view day trading like gambling, it is recommended that you create a trading strategy to be fully equipped with your fight. Every trader must have a plan to assist you in advance from the beginning point to the endpoint of your day trading goals. It will function as your map to demonstrate which courses are great to walk into and which courses to avoid.

- **Handle monetary resources.**

Many day traders stop working due to their inability to manage their finances correctly. It is not everything about providing money; it is about winning by thinking, if you observe that the market fall below fulfilling your possibilities of gaining revenue, then it is time to think fast of methods to prevent losses.

- **Offer short-term stock.**

This is done to avoid connecting weak stocks to your capital. By doing so, you will prevent any mistakes over your capital. If you have stocks which are most likely to hurl for over 25 % on the first three trading days, it is sensible to offer half of it. According to market pattern studies, if you sell any stock which tosses 25 % or even more throughout the first three days, you are more likely to gain earnings.

Day trading methods are everywhere. All you require to do is patiently compile them within your bounds. From your strategy collection, it is a good idea to select which ones will be appropriate for you. You ought to not stop, though, continue looking for different strategies because the market varies, and it makes drastic changes.

Someone has appropriately stated you need to "handle what you fear, and then you put an end to this fear.".

There is no rational need to fear the marketplace, given that it can be an excellent income for you. With this, you have to find methods to get rid of challenges; we need technology for the success of the day.

## Basic Things You Do Daily When You Are Trading In The Stockmarket

The first important step to take is by checking the last nights closing share cost. [presuming you have begun buying already]If you were going to sell, has the share rate dropped or reached your pre-chosen exit point?

If the share rate decreased, was your stop loss triggered?

Always LIMIT your order to the rate you wish to pay. When this is done, and you depend on the date with your share portfolio, then you can progress to your next task.

After the trading of stocks is under control, you can then begin to determine your next trading opportunities.

After you have bought your brand-new stock, [at the best price possible obviously] When the stock has been sold, set your exit target rate objective, so you know how much profit you want to make. Do not be greedy. Then set your stop loss into place.

When you first begin off, depending on the volatility of the stock, keep a watchful eye on them. Try not to open too many stocks at a time, when you are just entering the trade. When you first begin off, one or two stocks are adequate.

# CONCLUSION

Thanks for making it with me throughout this publication. I hope it was able and useful to give you the tools you require to accomplish your objectives, whatever they might be on stock investing.

By now, you already have an excellent structure that can lead you to success. The next step is to apply every little thing that you have discovered.

Happy trading!